Light, Lean, & Low-Fat

Recipes from the Rice Council

PUBLICATIONS INTERNATIONAL, LTD.

FAVORITE ALL TIME RECIPES is a trademark of Publications International, Ltd.

Copyright © 1992 USA Rice Council. All rights reserved.

Recipes were developed and tested by USA Rice Council, a non-profit organization established to promote the consumption of U.S. grown rice.

This edition published by:
Publications International, Ltd.
7373 North Cicero Avenue
Lincolnwood, Illinois 60646

ISBN: 1-56173-966-9

Photography by Myron Beck

Pictured on front cover: Almond Brown Rice Stuffing
(see page 64)

Manufactured in U.S.A.

8   7   6   5   4   3   2   1

Light, Lean, & Low-Fat

Recipes from the Rice Council

The Good News Is...Rice

"The good news is..."

What a welcome phrase these days, especially when it brings easy-to-use information about health and fitness.

At the USA Rice Council the news keeps getting better. Now that we are urged to evaluate some old favorites in our diets to avoid health problems, we learn that rice not only maintains its position of esteem, it also is earning new praise. Here's a favorite we don't have to give up—a nutrition-savvy food that fits perfectly into our health-conscious lifestyles.

This versatile world-popular grain almost does it all. It is low in fat and calories and is cholesterol-free. And lately, consumers have discovered rice bran, another flavorful shortcut to great nutrition.

So, the good news is...
• All the recipes in this collection provide 30 percent or less of the calories from fat.
• Many of the recipes are low in sodium and cholesterol. Check the nutritional analysis included with each recipe.
• Most recipes can be prepared in 30 minutes or less.

Overall, these recipes demonstrate how rice remarkably combines with most other foods and can be served any time of day, from breakfast to formal dinner. Furthermore, rice comes in several types and forms. You'll never be bored!

THE THREE TYPES OF RICE

Long Grain: Long and slender, these grains are 4 to 5 times as long as they are wide. Cooked grains remain separate, light, and fluffy. The perfect choice for salad, side-dish, or main-dish recipes.

Medium Grain: Plump, but not round, when these are cooked, the grains are more moist and tender than long grain. Ideal for risottos, croquettes, molds, and desserts.

Short Grain: Almost round, the grains tend to cling together when cooked—just right for puddings.

FORMS OF RICE

Brown: Rice from which only the hull has been removed. When cooked, it has a slightly chewy texture and nut-like flavor. This is a natural source of rice bran.

Parboiled: Unmilled rice is soaked, steamed, and dried before milling. Nutrients stay within the grain. A favorite of chefs who like fluffy and separate results.

Precooked: Rice is cooked and dehydrated after milling. It takes less time to prepare than other forms.

Regular-Milled White Rice: The rice has been completely milled, removing the bran layers. Vitamins and minerals are added for enrichment.

Rice Bran: Previously used only by commercial bakers, rice bran now is available for home cooking. Rice bran is a sweet, nutty tasting product that ranges in color from tan to dark brown. When you add it to your favorite recipes—at only 16 calories per tablespoon—it boosts flavor, while adding important vitamins, minerals, and fiber. Great for toppings and as a replacement for up to ¼ of the flour called for in bread, muffin, or cookie recipes.

HOW TO PREPARE RICE:

1 cup uncooked rice	Liquid*	Cooking Time
Regular-milled long grain	1¾ to 2 cups	15 minutes
Regular-milled medium or short grain	1½ to 1¾ cups	15 minutes
Brown	2 to 2½ cups	45 to 50 minutes
Parboiled	2 to 2½ cups	20 to 25 minutes
Precooked	Follow package directions.	Follow package directions.
Flavored or seasoned mixes	Follow package directions.	Follow package directions.

Combine 1 cup rice, liquid (see chart above), 1 teaspoon salt (optional), and 1 tablespoon butter or margarine (optional) in 2- to 3-quart saucepan. Bring to a boil; stir once or twice. Reduce heat; cover and simmer. Cook according to time specified on chart. If rice is not quite tender or liquid is not absorbed, replace lid and cook 2 to 4 minutes longer. Fluff with fork.

Cooked rice may be stored in the refrigerator for up to one week or in the freezer for six months.

Liquids other than water that can be used include: chicken broth, beef broth, bouillon, consommé, tomato or vegetable juice (1 part water, 1 part juice), fruit juice, such as orange or apple (1 part water, 1 part juice).

MICROWAVE OVEN INSTRUCTIONS

Combine 1 cup rice, liquid (see chart), 1 teaspoon salt (optional), and 1 tablespoon butter or margarine (optional) in 2- to 3-quart deep microproof baking dish. Cover and cook on HIGH 5 minutes or until boiling. Reduce setting to MEDIUM (50% power) and cook 15 minutes (20 minutes for parboiled rice and 30 minutes for brown rice). Fluff with fork.

A Fit Beginning

Wake up to these light and healthy favorites!

Brunch Rice

1 teaspoon margarine	½ teaspoon salt
¾ cup shredded carrots	¼ teaspoon ground black
¾ cup diced green pepper	pepper
¾ cup (about 3 ounces) sliced	3 cups cooked brown rice
fresh mushrooms	½ cup (2 ounces) shredded
6 egg whites, beaten	Cheddar cheese
2 eggs, beaten	6 corn tortillas, warmed
½ cup skim milk	(optional)

Heat margarine in large skillet over medium-high heat until hot. Add carrots, green pepper, and mushrooms; cook 2 minutes. Combine egg whites, eggs, milk, salt, and black pepper in small bowl. Reduce heat to medium and pour egg mixture over vegetables. Continue stirring 1½ to 2 minutes. Add rice and cheese; stir to gently separate grains. Heat 2 minutes. Serve immediately or spoon mixture into warmed corn tortillas.

Makes 6 servings

To microwave: Heat margarine in 2- to 3-quart microproof baking dish. Add carrots, green pepper, and mushrooms; cover and cook on HIGH 4 minutes. Combine egg whites, eggs, milk, salt, and black pepper in small bowl; pour over vegetables. Cook on HIGH 4 minutes, stirring with fork after each minute to cut cooked eggs into small pieces. Stir in rice and cheese; cook on HIGH about 1 minute or until thoroughly heated. Serve immediately or spoon mixture into warmed corn tortillas.

Each serving provides 212 calories, 11.4 grams protein, 6.5 grams fat, 27.0 grams carbohydrate, 2.5 grams dietary fiber, 353 milligrams sodium, and 79 milligrams cholesterol.

Brunch Rice

Breakfast in a Cup

3 cups cooked rice
1 cup (4 ounces) shredded Cheddar cheese, divided
1 can (4 ounces) diced green chiles
1 jar (2 ounces) diced pimientos, drained
⅓ cup skim milk
2 eggs, beaten
½ teaspoon ground cumin
½ teaspoon salt
½ teaspoon ground black pepper
Vegetable cooking spray

Combine rice, ½ cup cheese, chiles, pimientos, milk, eggs, cumin, salt, and pepper in large bowl. Evenly divide mixture into 12 muffin cups coated with cooking spray. Sprinkle with remaining ½ cup cheese. Bake at 400° F. for 15 minutes or until set. *Makes 12 servings*

Each serving provides 123 calories, 5.2 grams protein, 4.2 grams fat, 15.8 grams carbohydrate, 0.4 gram dietary fiber, 368 milligrams sodium, and 45 milligrams cholesterol.

Tip: Breakfast Cups may be stored in the freezer in freezer bag or tightly sealed container. To reheat frozen Breakfast Cups, microwave each cup on HIGH 1 minute.

Rice Bran Granola Cereal

2 cups uncooked old-fashioned rolled oats
1 cup crisp rice cereal
¾ cup rice bran
¾ cup raisins
⅓ cup slivered almonds
1 tablespoon ground cinnamon
⅓ cup honey
1 tablespoon margarine, melted
Vegetable cooking spray

Combine oats, cereal, bran, raisins, almonds, and cinnamon in large bowl; stir in honey and margarine. Spread mixture on baking sheet coated with cooking spray. Bake in preheated 350° F. oven for 8 to 10 minutes. Let cool. Serve as a topping for yogurt and/or fresh fruit. Store in a tightly covered container. *Makes 10 (½ cup) servings*

Each serving provides 199 calories, 5.0 grams protein, 6.6 grams fat, 34.5 grams carbohydrate, 4.4 grams dietary fiber, 57 milligrams sodium, and 0 milligram cholesterol.

Tip: Can be served as a cereal (with milk), or as a snack.

Raisin Rice Bran Muffins

1¼ cups whole-wheat flour
¾ cup rice bran
¾ cup raisins
½ cup sugar
2 teaspoons baking powder
1 teaspoon ground cinnamon
½ teaspoon salt
1¼ cups buttermilk
3 tablespoons vegetable oil
2 egg whites, lightly beaten
Vegetable cooking spray

Combine flour, bran, raisins, sugar, baking powder, cinnamon, and salt in large bowl. Combine buttermilk, oil, and egg whites in small bowl; add to dry ingredients. Stir just until dry ingredients are moistened. Spoon batter into 12 muffin cups coated with cooking spray. Bake at 400° F. for 15 to 17 minutes. Cool slightly on wire rack. Serve warm.

Makes 12 muffins

Each muffin provides 162 calories, 4.1 grams protein, 5.0 grams fat, 28.7 grams carbohydrate, 3.2 grams dietary fiber, 185 milligrams sodium, and 1 milligram cholesterol.

Tip: Muffins may be stored in the freezer in freezer bag or tightly sealed container. To reheat frozen muffins, microwave each muffin on HIGH 30 to 40 seconds or heat at 350°F. for 12 to 15 minutes.

Banana Pancakes

1 cup all-purpose flour
1 tablespoon sugar
1 teaspoon baking powder
½ teaspoon baking soda
½ teaspoon salt
1 container (6 ounces) banana custard-style yogurt
½ cup skim milk
1 egg, beaten
2 tablespoons vegetable oil
1 cup cooked rice
1 cup puréed or finely diced banana
Vegetable cooking spray

Combine flour, sugar, baking powder, baking soda, and salt in large bowl. Add yogurt, milk, egg, and oil; stir until smooth. Stir in rice and banana. Pour ¼ cup batter onto hot griddle coated with cooking spray. Cook over medium heat until bubbles form on top and underside is lightly browned. Turn to brown other side.

Makes 12 (4-inch) pancakes

Variation: For Cinnamon-Banana Pancakes, add ¼ teaspoon ground cinnamon to dry ingredients.

Each pancake provides 123 calories, 3.2 grams protein, 3.2 grams fat, 20.3 grams carbohydrate, 0.7 gram dietary fiber, 241 milligrams sodium, and 21 milligrams cholesterol.

Brown Rice, Mushroom, and Ham Hash

1 tablespoon olive oil
2 cups (about 8 ounces) sliced fresh mushrooms
1 small onion, minced
1 clove garlic, minced
3 cups cooked brown rice
1 cup (6 ounces) diced turkey ham
½ cup chopped walnuts (optional)
¼ cup snipped parsley
1 tablespoon white wine vinegar
1 tablespoon Dijon mustard
¼ teaspoon ground black pepper

Heat oil in Dutch oven or large saucepan over medium-low heat until hot. Add mushrooms, onion, and garlic; cook until tender. Stir in rice, ham, walnuts, parsley, vinegar, mustard, and pepper; cook, stirring until thoroughly heated. *Makes 8 servings*

To microwave: Combine oil, mushrooms, onion, and garlic in 2- to 3-quart microproof baking dish. Cook on HIGH 3 to 4 minutes. Stir in rice, ham, walnuts, parsley, vinegar, mustard, and pepper. Cook on HIGH 3 to 4 minutes, stirring after 2 minutes, or until thoroughly heated.

Each serving provides 133 calories, 6.2 grams protein, 3.5 grams fat, 19.6 grams carbohydrate, 1.9 grams dietary fiber, 184 milligrams sodium, and 10 milligrams cholesterol.

Brown Rice Griddle Cakes

1¾ cups buttermilk baking mix
½ cup rice bran
½ to 1 teaspoon ground cinnamon
1 cup skim milk
4 egg whites, lightly beaten
1½ cups cooked brown rice
¾ cup unsweetened applesauce
Vegetable cooking spray
Reduced-calorie syrup (optional)
Margarine (optional)

Combine baking mix, bran, cinnamon, milk, and egg whites in large bowl; stir until smooth. Stir in rice and applesauce. Pour ¼ cup batter onto hot griddle coated with cooking spray. Cook over medium heat until bubbles form on top and underside is lightly browned. Turn to brown other side. Serve with syrup and margarine.

Makes about 18 (4-inch) pancakes

Each pancake provides 85 calories, 3.1 grams protein, 0.9 gram fat, 16.7 grams carbohydrate, 1.3 grams dietary fiber, 207 milligrams sodium, and 0 milligram cholesterol.

Strawberry-Banana Smoothie

2 cups fresh or frozen
    unsweetened strawberries,
    hulled
2 bananas, sliced
1 container (8 ounces) low-fat
    vanilla yogurt

½ cup skim milk
¼ cup rice bran
3 tablespoons lemon juice
1 to 2 tablespoons honey

Cover and freeze strawberries and sliced bananas until firm, about 4 hours or overnight. Combine strawberries, bananas, yogurt, milk, bran, lemon juice, and honey in blender; process until smooth. Serve immediately in chilled glasses. *Makes 4 (1-cup) servings*

Each serving provides 168 calories, 5.6 grams protein, 2.4 grams fat, 35.3 grams carbohydrate, 4.0 grams dietary fiber, 55 milligrams sodium, and 3 milligrams cholesterol.

Praline Pancakes

1½ cups skim milk
2 tablespoons margarine,
    melted
2 teaspoons brandy
1 teaspoon vanilla extract
1 cup all-purpose flour
2 tablespoons sugar
1 teaspoon baking powder

¼ teaspoon salt
⅛ teaspoon ground cinnamon
1 cup cooked rice, cooled
⅓ cup pecans, coarsely chopped
4 egg whites, stiffly beaten
    Vegetable cooking spray
    Reduced-calorie syrup
    (optional)

Combine milk, margarine, brandy, vanilla, flour, sugar, baking powder, salt, and cinnamon in large bowl; stir until smooth. Stir in rice and pecans. Fold in beaten egg whites. Pour scant ¼ cup batter onto hot griddle coated with cooking spray. Cook over medium heat until bubbles form on top and underside is lightly browned. Turn to brown other side. Serve warm drizzled with syrup. *Makes 12 (4-inch) pancakes*

Each pancake provides 176 calories, 4.0 grams protein, 4.4 grams fat, 17.6 grams carbohydrate, .6 gram dietary fiber, 193.5 milligrams sodium, and .5 milligram cholesterol.

Strawberry-Banana Smoothies

Rice Bran Buttermilk Pancakes

1 cup rice flour or all-purpose
   flour
¾ cup rice bran
1 tablespoon sugar
1 teaspoon baking powder
½ teaspoon baking soda

1¼ cups low-fat buttermilk
3 egg whites, beaten
Vegetable cooking spray
Fresh fruit, reduced-calorie
   syrup or reduced-calorie
   margarine (optional)

Sift together flour, bran, sugar, baking powder, and baking soda into large bowl. Combine buttermilk and egg whites in small bowl; add to flour mixture. Stir until smooth. Pour ¼ cup batter onto hot griddle coated with cooking spray. Cook over medium heat until bubbles form on top and underside is lightly browned. Turn to brown other side. Serve with fresh fruit, syrup or margarine. *Makes about 10 (4-inch) pancakes*

Variation: For Cinnamon Pancakes, add 1 teaspoon ground cinnamon to dry ingredients.

Each pancake provides 99 calories, 3.9 grams protein, 2.0 grams fat, 18.1 grams carbohydrate, 2.1 grams dietary fiber, 119 milligrams sodium, and 1 milligram cholesterol.

Country Breakfast Cereal

3 cups cooked brown rice
2 cups skim milk
½ cup raisins or chopped
   prunes
1 tablespoon margarine
   (optional)

1 teaspoon ground cinnamon
⅛ teaspoon salt
Honey or brown sugar
   (optional)
Fresh fruit (optional)

Combine rice, milk, raisins, margarine, cinnamon, and salt in 2- to 3-quart saucepan. Bring to a boil; stir once or twice. Reduce heat to medium-low; cover and simmer 8 to 10 minutes or until thickened. Serve with honey and fresh fruit. *Makes 6 servings*

Each serving provides 174 calories, 5.7 grams protein, 1.1 grams fat, 36.2 grams carbohydrate, 2.4 grams dietary fiber, 98 milligrams sodium, and 2 milligrams cholesterol.

Rice Bran Buttermilk Pancakes

Light Previews

Start out your party or meal in a light way with these tempting recipes!

Cucumber Canapés

1 cup cooked rice, cooled to room temperature
1 large tomato, peeled and diced
½ cup chopped parsley
⅓ cup sliced green onions
¼ cup chopped mint
2 cloves garlic, minced

3 tablespoons plain nonfat yogurt*
1 tablespoon lemon juice
1 tablespoon olive oil
¼ teaspoon ground white pepper
2 to 3 large cucumbers, peeled

Combine rice, tomato, parsley, onions, mint, garlic, yogurt, lemon juice, oil, and pepper in large bowl. Cover and chill. Cut each cucumber crosswise into ½-inch slices; hollow out center of each slice, leaving bottom intact. Fill each cucumber slice with scant tablespoon rice mixture.
Makes about 3 dozen canapés

Substitute low-fat sour cream for yogurt, if desired.

Each serving (1 canapé) provides 17 calories, 0.5 gram protein, 0.5 gram fat, 2.9 grams carbohydrate, 0.3 gram dietary fiber, 26 milligrams sodium, and 0 milligram cholesterol.

Tip: Use ½ teaspoon measuring spoon to scoop seeds from cucumber.

Cucumber Canapés

Carrot-Rice Soup

1 pound carrots, peeled and
chopped
1 medium onion, chopped
1 tablespoon margarine
4 cups chicken broth, divided
¼ teaspoon dried tarragon
leaves

¼ teaspoon ground white
pepper
2¼ cups cooked rice
¼ cup light sour cream
Snipped parsley or mint for
garnish

Cook carrots and onion in margarine in large saucepan or Dutch oven
over medium-high heat 2 to 3 minutes or until onion is tender. Add
2 cups broth, tarragon, and pepper. Reduce heat; simmer 10 minutes.
Combine vegetables and broth in food processor or blender; process until
smooth. Return to saucepan. Add remaining 2 cups broth and rice;
thoroughly heat. Dollop sour cream on each serving of soup. Garnish
with parsley.   *Makes 6 servings*

Each serving provides 183 calories, 6.4 grams protein, 3.2 grams fat, 31.6 grams
carbohydrate, 3.2 grams dietary fiber, 860 milligrams sodium, and 0 milligram
cholesterol.

Pumpkin and Rice Soup

1 medium onion, chopped
1 clove garlic, minced
1 tablespoon vegetable oil
4 cups chicken broth
1 can (16 ounces) pumpkin
½ to 1 cup finely grated fresh
pumpkin* (optional)

½ teaspoon ground coriander
¼ to ½ teaspoon red pepper
flakes
¼ teaspoon ground nutmeg
3 cups hot cooked rice
Cilantro sprigs for garnish

Cook onion and garlic in oil in large saucepan or Dutch oven over
medium heat until onion is tender. Stir in broth, pumpkin, fresh
pumpkin, coriander, pepper flakes, and nutmeg. Bring to a boil. Reduce
heat; simmer, uncovered, 5 to 10 minutes. Top each serving with ½ cup
rice. Garnish with cilantro sprigs.   *Makes 6 servings*

*Substitute fresh acorn, butternut, hubbard, or other winter squash for fresh
pumpkin, if desired.*

Each serving provides 215 calories, 7.2 grams protein, 3.8 grams fat, 37.6 grams
carbohydrate, 2.2 grams dietary fiber, 913 milligrams sodium, and 0 milligram
cholesterol.

Pizza Rice Cakes

6 rice cakes	¼ cup (about 1 ounce) sliced
⅓ cup pizza sauce	fresh mushrooms
¼ cup sliced ripe olives	¼ cup (1 ounce) shredded
¼ cup diced green pepper	mozzarella cheese

Place rice cakes on baking sheet. Spread pizza sauce evenly on each rice cake; top with remaining ingredients. Bake at 400° F. for 10 minutes. Serve immediately.   *Makes 6 servings*

To microwave: Prepare rice cakes as directed on microproof baking sheet or plate. Cook, uncovered, on HIGH 1½ minutes; rotate after 1 minute. Serve immediately.

Each serving provides 64 calories, 2.0 grams protein, 2.1 grams fat, 9.7 grams carbohydrate, 0.5 gram dietary fiber, 110 milligrams sodium, and 4 milligrams cholesterol.

Tip: Makes a quick and easy after school snack; great for quick lunches, too!

Sherried Black Bean Soup

2 cans (16 ounces each) black beans, drained	½ cup rice bran (optional)
1½ cups water	¼ teaspoon ground black pepper
1 medium onion, chopped	1 tablespoon dry sherry
1 cup sliced celery	3 cups hot cooked brown rice
1 cup diced carrots	½ cup sliced green onions for garnish
1 tablespoon olive oil	½ cup finely chopped tomato for garnish
2 cups chicken broth	
1 can (4 ounces) diced green chiles	

Reserve 1 cup black beans. Place remaining beans and water in food processor or blender; process until smooth. Cook onion, celery, and carrots in oil in Dutch oven over medium-high heat until tender crisp. Add broth, chiles, bran, pepper, and whole and puréed beans. Reduce heat; simmer, uncovered, 10 to 15 minutes. Remove from heat; stir in sherry. Top each serving with ½ cup rice. Garnish with green onions and tomato.   *Makes 6 (1⅓-cup) servings*

Each serving provides 347 calories, 17.0 grams protein, 4.5 grams fat, 61.2 grams carbohydrate, 9.3 grams dietary fiber, 552 milligrams sodium, and 0 milligram cholesterol.

Rice Cubes with Satay Sauce

5¼ cups water, divided
2½ cups uncooked rice
1 teaspoon salt
¾ cup crunchy peanut butter
⅔ cup plain low-fat yogurt
⅓ cup chopped green onions

¼ cup lemon juice
2 tablespoons honey
2 tablespoons soy sauce
1 teaspoon ground ginger
½ teaspoon ground red pepper

Combine 5 cups water, rice, and salt in large saucepan; bring to a boil. Reduce heat; cover and simmer 20 to 25 minutes or until rice is tender and liquid is absorbed. Do not stir. Line 8×8×2-inch baking pan with plastic wrap; spread cooked rice evenly in pan. Cover with second piece of plastic wrap. Using bottom of another 8×8×2-inch baking pan, firmly press down rice. Remove empty pan; chill until rice is cold and firm.

To make Satay Sauce, combine peanut butter, yogurt, onions, lemon juice, remaining ¼ cup water, honey, soy sauce, ginger, and pepper in small bowl; stir until smooth. Cover and chill until ready to serve.

Remove plastic wrap from rice; invert pan. Remove plastic wrap lining; using a sharp knife, cut rice into 1-inch squares. Serve with sauce.

Makes 64 (1-inch) cubes

Each serving (1 cube and about 2 teaspoons sauce) provides 48 calories, 1.4 grams protein, 1.6 grams fat, 7.3 grams carbohydrate, 0.3 gram dietary fiber, 79 milligrams sodium, and 0 milligram cholesterol.

Spinach Rice Balls

2 cups cooked rice
1 package (10 ounces) frozen
    chopped spinach, thawed
    and squeezed dry*
⅔ cup dry Italian-style bread
    crumbs, divided

½ cup grated Parmesan cheese
⅓ cup minced onion
3 egg whites, beaten
¼ cup skim milk
1 tablespoon Dijon mustard
    Vegetable cooking spray

Combine rice, spinach, ⅓ cup bread crumbs, cheese, onion, egg whites, milk, and mustard in large bowl. Shape into 1-inch balls. Roll each ball in remaining ⅓ cup bread crumbs. Place on baking sheet coated with cooking spray. Bake at 375° F. for 10 to 15 minutes. Serve warm.

Makes about 3 dozen rice balls

Substitute 1 package (10 ounces) frozen chopped broccoli, thawed and well drained, for the spinach, if desired.

Each spinach ball provides 32 calories, 1.6 grams protein, 0.5 gram fat, 5.3 grams carbohydrate, 0.4 gram dietary fiber, 102 milligrams sodium, and 1 milligram cholesterol.

Cheddar-Rice Patties

2 cups cooked rice
1 cup (4 ounces) shredded
    low-fat Cheddar cheese
½ cup minced onion
3 tablespoons all-purpose
    flour
½ teaspoon salt
¼ teaspoon ground black
    pepper

3 egg whites
⅛ teaspoon cream of tartar
    Vegetable cooking spray
    Applesauce or apple wedges
    (optional)
    Low-fat sour cream
    (optional)

Combine rice, cheese, onion, flour, salt, and pepper in medium bowl.
Beat egg whites with cream of tartar in small bowl until stiff but not dry.
Fold beaten egg whites into rice mixture. Coat large skillet with cooking
spray and place over medium heat until hot. Spoon 2 to 3 tablespoons
batter into skillet for each patty; push batter into diamond shape using
spatula. Cook patties, turning once, until golden brown on both sides.
Serve warm with applesauce, apple wedges or sour cream.

Makes about 1 dozen (4 servings)

Each serving (3 patties) provides 233 calories, 14.2 grams protein, 6.4 grams fat,
29.3 grams carbohydrate, 2.2 grams dietary fiber, 550 milligrams sodium, and
18 milligrams cholesterol.

Tip: This recipe makes a great lunch item and is a favorite with kids!

Rice Cake De-Light

4 rice cakes
¼ cup light cream cheese,
    softened

¼ cup low-calorie fruit
    preserves

Top rice cakes with cream cheese, then with preserves.

Makes 4 servings

Variations: For Summer Fruit Rice Cakes, arrange on top of cakes with
cream cheese, 1 can (11 ounces) drained mandarin orange segments,
1 sliced kiwifruit, and ½ cup sliced strawberries.
For Rice Cake Treats, top rice cakes with 2 tablespoons smooth peanut
butter and 2 small sliced bananas.

Each serving provides 78 calories, 2.2 grams protein, 2.6 grams fat, 11.6 grams
carbohydrate, 0.1 gram dietary fiber, 84 milligrams sodium, and 8 milligrams
cholesterol.

Hearty Chicken and Rice Soup

10 cups chicken broth
1 medium onion, chopped
1 cup sliced celery
1 cup sliced carrots
¼ cup snipped parsley
½ teaspoon cracked black
  pepper

½ teaspoon dried thyme leaves
1 bay leaf
1½ cups chicken cubes (about
  ¾ pound)
2 cups cooked rice
2 tablespoons lime juice
  Lime slices for garnish

Combine broth, onion, celery, carrots, parsley, pepper, thyme, and bay leaf in Dutch oven. Bring to a boil; stir once or twice. Reduce heat; simmer, uncovered, 10 to 15 minutes. Add chicken; simmer, uncovered, 5 to 10 minutes or until chicken is cooked. Remove and discard bay leaf. Stir in rice and lime juice just before serving. Garnish with lime slices.

Makes 8 servings

Each serving provides 184 calories, 15.7 grams protein, 3.9 grams fat, 20.0 grams carbohydrate, 1.5 grams dietary fiber, 1209 milligrams sodium, and 23 milligrams cholesterol.

Seafood Gumbo

½ cup chopped onion
½ cup chopped green pepper
½ cup (about 2 ounces) sliced
  fresh mushrooms
1 clove garlic, minced
2 tablespoons margarine
1 can (28 ounces) whole
  tomatoes, undrained
2 cups chicken broth
½ to ¾ teaspoon ground red
  pepper

½ teaspoon dried thyme leaves
½ teaspoon dried basil leaves
1 package (10 ounces) frozen
  cut okra, thawed
¾ pound white fish, cut into
  1-inch pieces
½ pound peeled, deveined
  shrimp
3 cups hot cooked rice

Cook onion, green pepper, mushrooms, and garlic in margarine in large saucepan or Dutch oven over medium-high heat until tender crisp. Stir in tomatoes and juice, broth, red pepper, thyme, and basil. Bring to a boil. Reduce heat; simmer, uncovered, 10 to 15 minutes. Stir in okra, fish, and shrimp; simmer until fish flakes with fork, 5 to 8 minutes. Serve rice on top of gumbo.

Makes 6 servings

Each serving provides 328 calories, 25.0 grams protein, 6.9 grams fat, 41.1 grams carbohydrate, 2.5 grams dietary fiber, 987 milligrams sodium, and 64 milligrams cholesterol.

Mexican Rice Cakes

½ cup pinto beans, mashed
¼ teaspoon garlic powder
1 teaspoon lime juice
4 rice cakes

¼ cup picante sauce
¼ cup (1 ounce) shredded
    Cheddar cheese
¼ cup sliced jalapeño peppers*

Combine mashed beans with garlic powder and lime juice in small bowl. Spread mixture evenly on each rice cake; top with picante sauce, cheese, then peppers. Place rice cakes on baking sheet. Bake at 400° F. for 10 minutes. Serve immediately. *Makes 4 servings*

To microwave: Prepare rice cakes as directed on microproof baking sheet or plate. Cook, uncovered, on HIGH 1½ minutes; rotate after 1 minute. Serve immediately.

Substitute chopped green chiles for jalapeño peppers, if desired.

Each serving provides 106 calories, 4.8 grams protein, 2.7 grams fat, 15.9 grams carbohydrate, 1.2 grams dietary fiber, 211 milligrams sodium, and 7 milligrams cholesterol.

Tortilla Rice Soup

⅓ cup sliced green onions
    Vegetable cooking spray
4 cups chicken broth
2 cups cooked rice
1 can (10½ ounces) diced
    tomatoes with green
    chiles,* undrained
1 cup cooked chicken breast
    cubes

1 can (4 ounces) chopped
    green chiles
    Salt to taste (optional)
1 tablespoon lime juice
    Tortilla chips
½ cup chopped tomato
½ avocado, cut into small cubes
4 lime slices for garnish
    Cilantro sprigs for garnish

Cook onions in Dutch oven or large saucepan coated with cooking spray over medium-high heat until tender. Add broth, rice, tomatoes, chicken, and chiles. Reduce heat; cover and simmer 20 minutes. Stir in salt and lime juice. Just before serving, pour into soup bowls; top with tortilla chips, chopped tomato, and avocado. Garnish with lime slices and cilantro sprigs. *Makes 4 servings*

Look for diced tomatoes with green chiles in the Mexican food section of your supermarket.

Each serving provides 307 calories, 19.5 grams protein, 8.3 grams fat, 37.8 grams carbohydrate, 2.4 grams dietary fiber, 1403 milligrams sodium, and 31 milligrams cholesterol.

Mushroom and Rice Soup

2 cups (about 8 ounces) sliced
    fresh mushrooms
1 cup (about 4 ounces)
    chopped fresh mushrooms
1 cup sliced green onions
2 tablespoons olive oil
6 cups chicken broth
2 jars (7 ounces each) whole
    straw mushrooms,
    undrained

1 cup water
¾ teaspoon cracked black
    pepper
¾ teaspoon dried thyme leaves
3 cups cooked rice
1 tablespoon dry sherry

Cook sliced and chopped mushrooms and onions in oil in Dutch oven over medium-high heat until tender crisp. Add broth, straw mushrooms, water, pepper, and thyme. Reduce heat; simmer, uncovered, 5 to 7 minutes. Stir in rice and sherry; simmer 1 to 2 minutes. *Makes 10 servings*

Each serving provides 142 calories, 5.9 grams protein, 3.8 grams fat, 20.4 grams carbohydrate, 1.1 grams dietary fiber, 861 milligrams sodium, and 0 milligram cholesterol.

Chicken Pâté

1½ cups cooked chicken
½ cup cooked rice
2 tablespoons brandy
1 tablespoon chopped onion
1 tablespoon chopped chives
1 teaspoon Worcestershire
    sauce
½ teaspoon salt
½ teaspoon poultry seasoning
½ teaspoon rubbed sage

Vegetable cooking spray
    (optional)
Lettuce leaves
Paprika
Sliced red onion rings for
    garnish
Sliced ripe olives for garnish
Chutney
Miniature rice cakes or
    melba rounds

Combine chicken, rice, brandy, onion, chives, Worcestershire sauce, salt, poultry seasoning, and sage in food processor or blender; process until smooth. Shape mixture into round shape or fill small decorative mold coated with cooking spray. Cover and chill 1 to 2 hours or until ready to serve. Serve pâté on lettuce leaves. Sprinkle with paprika and garnish with red onion rings and olives. Serve with chutney on rice cakes or melba rounds. *Makes 2 cups*

Each serving (2 tablespoons) provides 38 calories, 4.0 grams protein, 1.0 gram fat, 2.0 grams carbohydrate, 0.1 gram dietary fiber, 112 milligrams sodium, and 12 milligrams cholesterol.

Turning a New Leaf

What better way to begin a healthy eating plan than by turning a new leaf with these tasty salads!

Curried Tuna Salad

3 cups hot cooked rice
½ cup frozen peas
1 to 2 cans (6½ ounces each) tuna, packed in water, drained and flaked
¾ cup chopped celery
¼ cup sliced green onions
1 tablespoon drained capers (optional)

¼ cup lemon juice
2 tablespoons olive oil
¼ teaspoon curry powder
¼ teaspoon hot pepper sauce
Shredded romaine lettuce
2 medium tomatoes, cut into wedges, for garnish

Combine hot rice and peas in large bowl; toss lightly. Add tuna, celery, onions, and capers. Combine lemon juice, oil, curry powder, and pepper sauce in small jar with lid. Pour over rice mixture; toss lightly. Cover and chill 30 minutes. Serve on shredded lettuce and garnish with tomato wedges.

Makes 6 servings

Each serving provides 245 calories, 13.1 grams protein, 5.8 grams fat, 34.6 grams carbohydrate, 2.6 grams dietary fiber, 551 milligrams sodium, and 13 milligrams cholesterol.

Curried Tuna Salad

Black Bean and Rice Salad

2 cups cooked rice, cooled to
    room temperature
1 cup cooked black beans*
1 medium tomato, seeded and
    chopped
½ cup (2 ounces) shredded
    Cheddar cheese (optional)

1 tablespoon snipped parsley
¼ cup prepared light Italian
    dressing
1 tablespoon lime juice
Lettuce leaves

Combine rice, beans, tomato, cheese, and parsley in large bowl. Pour
dressing and lime juice over rice mixture; toss lightly. Serve on lettuce
leaves.   *Makes 4 servings*

Substitute canned black beans, drained, for the cooked beans, if desired.

Each serving provides 210 calories, 7.4 grams protein, 0.7 gram fat, 43.1 grams
carbohydrate, 3.2 grams dietary fiber, 560 milligrams sodium, and 0 milligram
cholesterol.

Gazpacho Salad

3 cups cooked rice, cooled to
    room temperature
2 large tomatoes, cut into
    wedges
1 cup (about 4 ounces) sliced
    fresh mushrooms
1 medium green pepper, cut
    into strips
⅓ cup sliced green onions
1 tablespoon snipped parsley
    or cilantro

2 tablespoons vegetable oil
2 tablespoons white vinegar
1 tablespoon snipped basil
    leaves*
1 clove garlic, minced
¼ teaspoon salt
¼ teaspoon ground black
    pepper
Lettuce leaves

Combine rice, tomatoes, mushrooms, green pepper, onions, and parsley
in large bowl. Combine oil, vinegar, basil, garlic, salt, and black pepper in
small jar with lid. Pour over rice mixture; toss lightly. Serve on lettuce
leaves.   *Makes 6 servings*

Substitute ¼ teaspoon dried basil for fresh basil, if desired.

Each serving provides 189 calories, 3.6 grams protein, 5.0 grams fat, 32.4 grams
carbohydrate, 1.6 grams dietary fiber, 494 milligrams sodium, and 0 milligram
cholesterol.

Black Bean and Rice Salad

Grilled Chicken Salad

¾ pound boned and skinned
   chicken breast
½ teaspoon salt
½ teaspoon ground black
   pepper
1½ cups diagonally sliced small
   zucchini
3 cups cooked rice, cooled to
   room temperature
1 can (14 ounces) artichoke
   hearts, drained

¾ cup fresh snow peas,
   blanched*
½ medium red pepper, cut into
   1-inch cubes
⅓ cup light Italian salad
   dressing
1 teaspoon chopped fresh basil
   leaves
Lettuce leaves

Season chicken with salt and black pepper. Grill or broil chicken breast. Add zucchini during last 5 minutes of grilling or broiling. Cover and chill chicken and zucchini; cut chicken in ¾-inch cubes. Combine rice, chicken, zucchini, artichokes, snow peas, and red pepper in large bowl. Blend dressing and basil in small bowl. Pour over salad; toss lightly. Serve on lettuce leaves. *Makes 4 servings*

Substitute frozen snow peas, thawed, for fresh snow peas, if desired.

Each serving provides 416 calories, 34.3 grams protein, 3.8 grams fat, 60.2 grams carbohydrate, 3.0 grams dietary fiber, 1227 milligrams sodium, and 72 milligrams cholesterol.

Marinated Vegetable Salad

1 cup (about 4 ounces) sliced
   fresh mushrooms
¾ cup halved cherry tomatoes
½ cup avocado chunks
   (optional)
½ cup sliced ripe olives
⅓ cup chopped red onion
3 tablespoons red wine vinegar

2 tablespoons olive oil
1 tablespoon snipped parsley
½ teaspoon sugar
¼ teaspoon salt
¼ teaspoon dried basil leaves
3 cups cooked rice, cooled
   Red onion rings for garnish

Combine mushrooms, tomatoes, avocado, olives, and onion in shallow dish. Combine vinegar, oil, parsley, sugar, salt, and basil in jar with lid. Pour over vegetables. Cover and chill 2 to 3 hours. Add rice; toss lightly. Garnish with red onion rings. *Makes 8 servings*

Each serving provides 148 calories, 2.6 grams protein, 4.6 grams fat, 24.3 grams carbohydrate, 1.1 grams dietary fiber, 443 milligrams sodium, and 0 milligram cholesterol.

Grilled Chicken Salad

Refreshing Turkey Salad

3 cups cooked rice, cooled to
  room temperature
2 cups diced cantaloupe
1½ cups cooked turkey breast
  cubes
¼ cup packed mint leaves
¼ cup packed parsley

1 clove garlic, halved
1 container (8 ounces) plain
  nonfat yogurt
Lettuce leaves
Assorted fresh fruit for
  garnish (optional)

Combine rice, cantaloupe, and turkey in large bowl. Finely chop mint,
parsley, and garlic in food processor. Add yogurt and blend. Add to rice
mixture; toss lightly. Cover and chill 2 hours. Serve on lettuce leaves.
Garnish with fresh fruit. *Makes 4 servings*

Each serving provides 332 calories, 24.2 grams protein, 1.2 grams fat, 54.5 grams
carbohydrate, 1.6 grams dietary fiber, 667 milligrams sodium, and 45 milligrams
cholesterol.

Shrimp and Strawberry Salad

3 cups cooked rice
½ pound peeled, deveined
  cooked small shrimp
¾ cup thinly sliced celery
⅔ cup cholesterol free, reduced
  calorie mayonnaise
½ cup low-fat strawberry
  yogurt

1 teaspoon dry mustard
1 teaspoon lemon juice
½ teaspoon salt
1½ cups sliced fresh strawberries
  Romaine lettuce

Combine rice, shrimp, and celery in large bowl. Combine mayonnaise,
yogurt, mustard, lemon juice, and salt in medium bowl; mix well. Add
yogurt mixture to rice mixture and stir well. Fold in strawberries. Cover
and chill until serving time. Arrange lettuce on individual serving plates;
top with salad. *Makes 6 servings*

Each serving provides 274 calories, 10.4 grams protein, 9.2 grams fat, 36.6 grams
carbohydrate, 1.8 grams dietary fiber, 833 milligrams sodium, and 69 milligrams
cholesterol.

Paella Salad

2 cups cooked rice (cooked in chicken broth and ⅛ teaspoon saffron*)
1 cup cooked chicken breast cubes
1 cup peeled, deveined cooked shrimp
1 medium tomato, seeded and diced
½ cup chopped onion
⅓ cup cooked green peas
⅓ cup sliced ripe olives
3 tablespoons white wine vinegar
1 tablespoon olive oil
1 clove garlic, minced
½ teaspoon salt
½ teaspoon ground white pepper
Lettuce leaves

Combine rice, chicken, shrimp, tomato, onion, peas, and olives in large bowl. Combine vinegar, oil, garlic, salt, and pepper in jar with lid. Pour over rice mixture; toss lightly. Serve on lettuce leaves.

Makes 4 servings

Substitute ground turmeric for the saffron, if desired.

Each serving provides 288 calories, 23.5 grams protein, 7.0 grams fat, 31.3 grams carbohydrate, 1.9 grams dietary fiber, 770 milligrams sodium, and 99 milligrams cholesterol.

Santa Fe Salad

2 cups cooked brown rice, cooled
1 can (16 ounces) black beans or pinto beans, rinsed and drained
1 can (17 ounces) whole kernel corn, drained
¼ cup minced onion
¼ cup white vinegar
2 tablespoons vegetable oil
2 tablespoons snipped cilantro
2 jalapeño peppers, minced
2 teaspoons chili powder
1 teaspoon salt

Combine rice, beans, corn, and onion in medium bowl. Combine vinegar, oil, cilantro, peppers, chili powder, and salt in small jar with lid. Pour over rice mixture; toss lightly. Cover and chill 2 to 3 hours so flavors will blend. Stir before serving.

Makes 4 servings

Each serving provides 425 calories, 15.9 grams protein, 9.2 grams fat, 75.5 grams carbohydrate, 8.1 grams dietary fiber, 934 milligrams sodium, and 0 milligram cholesterol.

Stir-Fry Beef Salad

1 pound boneless beef sirloin
    steak
2 tablespoons olive oil, divided
1 tablespoon grated fresh
    ginger root
1 clove garlic, minced
1 small red onion, chopped
1 cup (about 4 ounces) fresh
    mushrooms, quartered

3 tablespoons cider vinegar
1 tablespoon soy sauce
1 tablespoon honey
3 cups hot cooked rice
½ pound fresh spinach, torn
    into bite-size pieces
1 medium tomato, seeded and
    coarsely chopped

Partially freeze steak; slice across the grain into ⅛-inch strips. Set aside.
Heat 1 tablespoon oil, ginger root, and garlic in large skillet or wok over
high heat until hot. Stir-fry beef (half at a time) 1 to 2 minutes. Remove
beef; keep warm. Add remaining 1 tablespoon oil; heat until hot. Add
onion and mushrooms; cook 1 to 2 minutes. Stir in vinegar, soy sauce,
and honey. Bring mixture to a boil. Add beef and rice; toss lightly. Serve
over spinach. Top with tomato; serve immediately. *Makes 6 servings*

Each serving provides 334 calories, 22.9 grams protein, 10.3 grams fat, 36.9 grams
carbohydrate, 2.8 grams dietary fiber, 602 milligrams sodium, and 53 milligrams
cholesterol.

Turkey Ensalada con Queso

2 cups cooked rice, cooled to
    room temperature
1½ cups cooked turkey breast
    cubes
½ cup (2 ounces) jalapeño
    Monterey Jack cheese cut
    into ½-inch cubes
1 can (4 ounces) diced green
    chiles

2 tablespoons snipped parsley
¼ cup cholesterol free, reduced
    calorie mayonnaise
¼ cup plain nonfat yogurt
    Lettuce leaves
    Tomato wedges for garnish

Combine rice, turkey, cheese, chiles, and parsley in large bowl. Blend
mayonnaise and yogurt; add to rice mixture and toss lightly. Serve on
lettuce leaves; garnish with tomato wedges. *Makes 4 servings*

Each serving provides 307 calories, 23.4 grams protein, 7.9 grams fat, 34.0 grams
carbohydrate, 0.9 gram dietary fiber, 581 milligrams sodium, and 59 milligrams
cholesterol.

Stir-Fry Beef Salad

Summer Fruit Salad

2 cups cooked rice, cooled to
    room temperature
½ cup quartered strawberries
½ cup grape halves
2 kiwifruit, sliced into
    quarters
½ cup pineapple tidbits

½ cup banana slices
¼ cup pineapple juice
2 tablespoons plain nonfat
    yogurt
1 tablespoon honey
Lettuce leaves

Combine rice and fruit in large bowl. Blend pineapple juice, yogurt, and
honey in small bowl. Pour over rice mixture; toss lightly. Serve on lettuce
leaves.   *Makes 4 servings*

Each serving provides 239 calories, 4.1 grams protein, 1.1 grams fat, 54.0 grams
carbohydrate, 3.1 grams dietary fiber, 396 milligrams sodium, and 1 milligram
cholesterol.

Chinese Chicken Salad

3 cups cooked rice, cooled
1 cup cooked chicken breast
    cubes
1 cup sliced celery
1 can (8 ounces) sliced water
    chestnuts, drained
1 cup fresh bean sprouts*
½ cup (about 2 ounces) sliced
    fresh mushrooms
¼ cup sliced green onions

¼ cup diced red pepper
3 tablespoons lemon juice
2 tablespoons reduced-sodium
    soy sauce
2 tablespoons sesame oil
2 teaspoons grated fresh
    ginger root
¼ to ½ teaspoon ground white
    pepper
Lettuce leaves

Combine rice, chicken, celery, water chestnuts, bean sprouts, mushrooms,
onions, and red pepper in large bowl. Combine lemon juice, soy sauce,
oil, ginger root, and white pepper in small jar with lid. Pour over rice
mixture; toss lightly. Serve on lettuce leaves.   *Makes 6 servings*

*Substitute canned bean sprouts, rinsed and drained, for fresh bean sprouts,
if desired.*

Each serving provides 248 calories, 11.6 grams protein, 5.8 grams fat, 37.1 grams
carbohydrate, 1.5 grams dietary fiber, 593 milligrams sodium, and 20 milligrams
cholesterol.

Summer Fruit Salad

Saffron Rice Salad

2½ cups cooked rice (cooked in chicken broth and ⅛ teaspoon saffron*), cooled to room temperature
½ cup diced red pepper
½ cup diced green pepper
¼ cup sliced green onions
¼ cup sliced ripe olives
2 tablespoons white wine vinegar
1 teaspoon olive oil
2 to 3 drops hot pepper sauce (optional)
1 clove garlic, minced
¼ teaspoon ground white pepper
Lettuce leaves

Combine rice, red and green peppers, onions, and olives in large bowl. Combine vinegar, oil, pepper sauce, garlic, and white pepper in jar with lid. Pour over rice mixture; toss lightly. Serve on lettuce leaves.

Makes 4 servings

Substitute ground turmeric for the saffron, if desired.

Each serving provides 177 calories, 5.2 grams protein, 3.0 grams fat, 31.8 grams carbohydrate, 1.4 grams dietary fiber, 416 milligrams sodium, and 0 milligram cholesterol.

Summer Seafood Salad

2 cups cooked rice, cooled to room temperature
½ pound cooked crabmeat*
1 can (8 ounces) sliced water chestnuts, drained
½ cup sliced celery
¼ cup sliced green onions
¼ cup plain nonfat yogurt
¼ cup light dairy sour cream
1 tablespoon lemon juice
¼ teaspoon hot pepper sauce
¼ teaspoon salt
Lettuce leaves
Tomato wedges for garnish

Combine rice, crabmeat, water chestnuts, celery, and onions in large bowl. Combine yogurt, sour cream, lemon juice, pepper sauce, and salt in small bowl; blend well. Pour over rice mixture; toss lightly. Serve on lettuce leaves and garnish with tomato wedges.

Makes 4 servings

Substitute surimi seafood, crab-flavored, flake or chunk style for the crabmeat, if desired.

Each serving provides 263 calories, 15.9 grams protein, 4.8 grams fat, 38.1 grams carbohydrate, 1.2 grams dietary fiber, 731 milligrams sodium, and 65 milligrams cholesterol.

Saffron Rice Salad

Sesame Pork Salad

3 cups cooked rice
1½ cups slivered cooked pork*
¼ pound fresh snow peas, trimmed and julienned
1 medium cucumber, peeled, seeded, and julienned
1 medium red pepper, julienned
½ cup sliced green onions

2 tablespoons sesame seeds, toasted (optional)
¼ cup chicken broth
3 tablespoons rice or white wine vinegar
3 tablespoons soy sauce
1 tablespoon peanut oil
1 teaspoon sesame oil

Combine rice, pork, snow peas, cucumber, pepper, onions, and sesame seeds in large bowl. Combine broth, vinegar, soy sauce, and oils in small jar with lid. Pour over rice mixture; toss lightly. Serve at room temperature or slightly chilled.   *Makes 6 servings*

Substitute 1½ cups slivered cooked chicken for pork, if desired.

Each serving provides 269 calories, 13.8 grams protein, 8.4 grams fat, 33.5 grams carbohydrate, 1.6 grams dietary fiber, 867 milligrams sodium, and 32 milligrams cholesterol.

Rice Salad Milano

3 cups hot cooked rice
2 tablespoons vegetable oil
2 tablespoons lemon juice
1 clove garlic, minced
½ teaspoon salt (optional)
½ teaspoon dried rosemary leaves
½ teaspoon dried oregano leaves

½ teaspoon ground black pepper
1 small zucchini, julienned*
1 medium tomato, seeded and chopped
2 tablespoons grated Parmesan cheese

Place rice in large bowl. Combine oil, lemon juice, garlic, salt, rosemary, oregano, and pepper in small jar with lid. Pour over rice; toss lightly. Cover; let cool. Add remaining ingredients. Serve at room temperature or chilled.   *Makes 6 servings*

To julienne, slice zucchini diagonally. Cut slices into matchstick-size strips.

Each serving provides 189 calories, 3.9 grams protein, 5.4 grams fat, 30.8 grams carbohydrate, 0.9 gram dietary fiber, 620 milligrams sodium, and 1 milligram cholesterol.

Sesame Pork Salad

Specialties of the House

Bring on the family or dinner guests and treat them to the specialties of the house using our versatile rice recipes.

Stuffed Chicken Breasts

4 boneless, skinless chicken breast halves (about 1 pound), pounded to ¼-inch thickness
½ teaspoon ground black pepper, divided
¼ teaspoon salt
1 cup cooked brown rice (cooked in chicken broth)
¼ cup minced tomato
¼ cup (1 ounce) finely shredded mozzarella cheese
3 tablespoons toasted rice bran* (optional)
1 tablespoon chopped fresh basil
Vegetable cooking spray

Season insides of chicken breasts with ¼ teaspoon pepper and salt. Combine rice, tomato, cheese, bran, basil, and remaining ¼ teaspoon pepper. Spoon rice mixture on top of pounded chicken breasts; fold over and secure sides with wooden toothpicks soaked in water. Wipe off outsides of chicken breasts with paper towel. Coat a large skillet with cooking spray and place over medium-high heat until hot. Cook stuffed chicken breasts 1 minute on each side or just until golden brown. Transfer chicken to shallow baking pan. Bake at 350° F. for 8 to 10 minutes.

Makes 4 servings

*To toast rice bran, spread on baking sheet and bake at 325°F. for 7 to 8 minutes.

Each serving provides 223 calories, 30.0 grams protein, 5.2 grams fat, 12.1 grams carbohydrate, 1.0 gram dietary fiber, 337 milligrams sodium, and 79 milligrams cholesterol.

Stuffed Chicken Breasts

Turkey and Rice Quiche

3 cups cooked rice, cooled to
    room temperature
1½ cups chopped cooked turkey
1 medium tomato, seeded and
    finely diced
¼ cup sliced green onions
¼ cup finely diced green pepper
1 tablespoon chopped fresh
    basil or 1 teaspoon
    dried basil

½ teaspoon seasoned salt
⅛ to ¼ teaspoon ground red
    pepper
½ cup skim milk
3 eggs, beaten
    Vegetable cooking spray
½ cup (2 ounces) shredded
    Cheddar cheese
½ cup (2 ounces) shredded
    mozzarella cheese

Combine rice, turkey, tomato, onions, green pepper, basil, salt, red
pepper, milk, and eggs in 13×9×2-inch pan coated with cooking spray.
Top with cheeses. Bake at 375° F. for 20 minutes or until knife inserted
near center comes out clean. To serve, cut quiche into 8 squares; cut each
square diagonally into 2 triangles.   *Makes 8 servings (2 triangles each)*

Each serving provides 231 calories, 16.1 grams protein, 7.4 grams fat, 23.9 grams
carbohydrate, 0.8 gram dietary fiber, 527 milligrams sodium, and 111 milligrams
cholesterol.

Vegetable Pork Stir-Fry

¾ pound pork tenderloin
1 tablespoon vegetable oil
1½ cups (about 6 ounces) sliced
    fresh mushrooms
1 large green pepper, cut into
    strips
1 zucchini, thinly sliced
2 ribs celery, cut into diagonal
    slices

1 cup thinly sliced carrots
1 clove garlic, minced
1 cup chicken broth
2 tablespoons reduced-sodium
    soy sauce
1½ tablespoons cornstarch
3 cups hot cooked rice

Slice pork across the grain into ⅛-inch strips. Brown pork strips in oil in
large skillet over medium-high heat. Push meat to side of skillet. Add
mushrooms, pepper, zucchini, celery, carrots, and garlic; stir-fry about
3 minutes. Combine broth, soy sauce, and cornstarch. Add to skillet and
cook, stirring, until thickened; cook 1 minute longer. Serve over rice.

Makes 6 servings

Each serving provides 257 calories, 16.8 grams protein, 4.4 grams fat, 36.3 grams
carbohydrate, 2.1 grams dietary fiber, 732 milligrams sodium, and 37 milligrams
cholesterol.

Turkey and Rice Quiche

Sherried Beef

¾ pound boneless beef top
round steak
1 cup water
¼ cup dry sherry
3 tablespoons soy sauce
2 large carrots, cut into
diagonal slices

1 large green pepper, cut into
strips
1 medium onion, cut into
chunks
2 tablespoons vegetable oil,
divided
1 tablespoon cornstarch
2 cups hot cooked rice

Partially freeze steak; slice across the grain into ⅛-inch strips. Combine water, sherry, and soy sauce. Pour over beef in dish; marinate 1 hour. Stir-fry vegetables in 1 tablespoon oil in large skillet over medium-high heat. Remove from skillet; set aside. Drain beef; reserve marinade. Brown beef in remaining 1 tablespoon oil. Combine cornstarch with marinade in bowl. Add vegetables and marinade to beef. Cook, stirring, until sauce is thickened; cook 1 minute longer. Serve over rice.   *Makes 4 servings*

Each serving provides 365 calories, 23.9 grams protein, 10.9 grams fat, 41.5 grams carbohydrate, 3.3 grams dietary fiber, 1080 milligrams sodium, and 48 milligrams cholesterol.

Curried Black Beans and Rice with Sausage

1 tablespoon olive oil
1 medium onion, minced
1 tablespoon curry powder
½ pound smoked turkey
sausage, thinly sliced
¾ cup chicken broth

2 cans (16 ounces each) black
beans, drained
1 tablespoon white wine
vinegar (optional)
3 cups cooked rice

Heat oil in large heavy skillet over medium heat. Cook onion and curry powder, stirring well, until tender. Stir in sausage and broth; simmer 5 minutes. Stir in beans; cook until hot, stirring constantly. Remove from heat and stir in vinegar. Spoon over rice.   *Makes 10 servings*

To microwave: Combine oil, onion, and curry powder in 2- to 3-quart microproof baking dish. Cook on HIGH 2 minutes or until onion is tender. Add sausage, broth, and beans; cover with plastic wrap and cook on HIGH 5 to 6 minutes, stirring after 3 minutes, or until thoroughly heated. Continue as directed above.

Each serving provides 267 calories, 14.1 grams protein, 5.4 grams fat, 41.0 grams carbohydrate, 4.7 grams dietary fiber, 481 milligrams sodium, and 16 milligrams cholesterol.

Sherried Beef

Shrimp La Louisiana

1 tablespoon margarine
1½ cups uncooked rice*
1 medium onion, chopped
1 green pepper, chopped
2¾ cups beef broth
¼ teaspoon salt
¼ teaspoon ground black
  pepper

¼ teaspoon hot pepper sauce
1 pound medium shrimp,
  peeled and deveined
1 can (4 ounces) sliced
  mushrooms, drained
3 tablespoons snipped parsley
¼ cup sliced green onions for
  garnish (optional)

Melt margarine in 3-quart saucepan. Add rice, onion, and green pepper. Cook 2 to 3 minutes. Add broth, salt, black pepper, and pepper sauce; bring to a boil. Cover and simmer 15 minutes. Add shrimp, mushrooms, and parsley. Cook 5 minutes longer or until shrimp turn pink. Garnish with green onions. *Makes 8 servings*

Recipe based on regular-milled long grain white rice. If using other types of rice, refer to chart on page 5 for adjustments of liquid and time.

Each serving provides 206 calories, 14.1 grams protein, 2.5 grams fat, 31.0 grams carbohydrate, 1.0 gram dietary fiber, 527 milligrams sodium, and 96 milligrams cholesterol.

Rice-Stuffed Fish Fillets with Mushroom Sauce

3 cups cooked rice
¼ cup diced pimientos
2 tablespoons snipped parsley
1 teaspoon grated lemon peel
¼ teaspoon salt
¼ teaspoon ground white
  pepper

1 pound white fish fillets*
  Vegetable cooking spray
2 teaspoons margarine, melted
½ teaspoon seasoned salt
¼ teaspoon paprika
  Lemon slices for garnish
  Mushroom Sauce (recipe
    follows)

Combine rice, pimientos, parsley, lemon peel, salt, and pepper in large bowl. Place fillets in shallow baking dish coated with cooking spray. Spoon rice mixture on lower portion of each fillet. Fold over to enclose rice mixture; fasten with wooden toothpicks soaked in water. Brush fillets with margarine; sprinkle with seasoned salt and paprika. Bake at 400° F. for 10 to 15 minutes or until fish flakes easily with fork. Prepare Mushroom Sauce while fillets are baking. Transfer fillets to serving platter; garnish platter with lemon slices. Serve fillets with Mushroom Sauce. *Makes 4 servings*

Haddock, orange roughy, sole, or turbot may be used.

continued

Mushroom Sauce

2 cups (about 8 ounces) sliced
    fresh mushrooms
½ cup sliced green onions
1 teaspoon margarine
½ cup water

⅓ cup white wine
1 tablespoon white wine
    Worcestershire sauce
½ cup cholesterol free, reduced
    calorie mayonnaise

Cook mushrooms and onions in margarine in large skillet until tender. Add water, wine, and Worcestershire sauce; bring to a boil. Reduce sauce slightly. Stir in mayonnaise; keep warm.

Each serving provides 440 calories, 27.0 grams protein, 14.0 grams fat, 49.6 grams carbohydrate, 1.8 grams dietary fiber, 1666 milligrams sodium, and 66 milligrams cholesterol.

Curried Scallops in Rice Ring

Vegetable cooking spray
1½ pounds bay scallops
1 tablespoon margarine
1 medium onion, chopped
1 teaspoon all-purpose flour
½ teaspoon salt
1 bottle (8 ounces) clam juice
1 cup evaporated skim milk

1 red apple, cored and chopped
½ teaspoon curry powder
6 cups hot cooked rice
1 tablespoon snipped parsley
1 tablespoon diced pimiento
    Chutney, chopped peanuts,
    grated coconut, and raisins
    for condiments (optional)

Coat large skillet with cooking spray and place over medium heat until hot. Add scallops; cook until scallops are almost done, 2 to 3 minutes. Remove scallops from skillet; keep warm. Melt margarine in skillet; add onion and cook 1 to 2 minutes or until tender. Stir in flour and salt; cook, stirring, 2 minutes over medium-high heat. Gradually add clam juice and milk, stirring constantly until thickened. Stir in scallops, apple, and curry powder. Keep warm. Combine rice, parsley, and pimiento; pack into 2-quart ring mold coated with cooking spray. Unmold onto serving platter and fill center of ring with curried scallops. Serve with chutney, chopped peanuts, grated coconut, and raisins.   *Makes 6 servings*

Each serving provides 440 calories, 28.4 grams protein, 3.6 grams fat, 70.7 grams carbohydrate, 2.2 grams dietary fiber, 1315 milligrams sodium, and 39 milligrams cholesterol.

Baked Stuffed Snapper

1 red snapper (1½ pounds)
2 cups hot cooked rice
1 can (4 ounces) sliced
    mushrooms, drained
½ cup diced water chestnuts
¼ cup thinly sliced green
    onions
¼ cup diced pimiento

2 tablespoons chopped parsley
1 tablespoon grated lemon peel
½ teaspoon salt
⅛ teaspoon ground black
    pepper
Vegetable cooking spray
1 tablespoon margarine,
    melted

Clean and butterfly fish. Combine rice, mushrooms, water chestnuts, onions, pimiento, parsley, lemon peel, salt, and pepper; toss lightly. Fill cavity of fish with rice mixture; enclose filling with wooden toothpicks soaked in water. Place fish in 13×9×2-inch baking dish coated with cooking spray; brush fish with margarine. Bake fish at 400° F. for 18 to 20 minutes or until fish flakes easily with fork. Wrap remaining rice in foil and bake in oven with fish. *Makes 4 servings*

Each serving provides 349 calories, 38.7 grams protein, 5.6 grams fat, 33.3 grams carbohydrate, 1.2 grams dietary fiber, 947 milligrams sodium, and 63 milligrams cholesterol.

Skillet Sauerbraten

¾ pound boneless beef sirloin
    steak
⅔ cup crushed gingersnaps
    (about 10 cookies)
½ teaspoon salt
1 tablespoon vegetable oil
1 medium onion, sliced

3 ribs celery, sliced
2 carrots, thinly sliced
1½ cups beef broth
⅓ cup cider vinegar
2 tablespoons cornstarch
2 tablespoons water
3 cups hot cooked brown rice

Partially freeze steak; slice diagonally across grain into ⅛-inch strips. Combine gingersnap crumbs and salt in medium bowl. Dredge slices into crumb mixture; set aside. Heat oil in large skillet over medium-high heat until hot. Add half of steak slices, stirring to brown both sides. Cook 2 minutes or until done. Reserve and keep warm. Repeat with remaining steak slices. Add onion, celery, and carrots to hot skillet; cook 5 minutes or until tender crisp. Add broth and vinegar; reduce heat and simmer 5 minutes. Combine cornstarch with water. Add to skillet, stirring constantly, until thickened; cook 1 minute longer. Add reserved steak slices; pour mixture over rice. *Makes 6 servings*

Each serving provides 309 calories, 18.8 grams protein, 8.0 grams fat, 40.1 grams carbohydrate, 3.2 grams dietary fiber, 470 milligrams sodium, and 51 milligrams cholesterol.

Baked Stuffed Snapper

Red Beans and Rice

Vegetable cooking spray
½ cup chopped onion
½ cup chopped celery
½ cup chopped green pepper
2 cloves garlic, minced
2 cans (15 ounces each) red beans,* drained
½ pound fully-cooked low-fat turkey sausage, cut into ¼-inch slices
1 can (8 ounces) tomato sauce
1 teaspoon Worcestershire sauce
¼ teaspoon ground red pepper
¼ teaspoon hot pepper sauce
3 cups hot cooked rice
Hot pepper sauce (optional)

Coat Dutch oven with cooking spray and place over medium-high heat until hot. Add onion, celery, green pepper, and garlic. Cook 2 to 3 minutes. Add beans, sausage, tomato sauce, Worcestershire sauce, red pepper, and pepper sauce. Reduce heat; cover and simmer 15 minutes. Serve beans with rice and pepper sauce.   *Makes 6 servings*

Substitute your favorite bean for the red beans, if desired.

Each serving provides 373 calories, 19.8 grams protein, 6.2 grams fat, 60.3 grams carbohydrate, 5.8 grams dietary fiber, 952 milligrams sodium, and 26 milligrams cholesterol.

Spring Lamb Skillet

2 teaspoons olive oil
1 pound boneless lamb, cut into 1-inch cubes
2 cups thinly sliced yellow squash
2 cups (about 8 ounces) sliced fresh mushrooms
2 medium tomatoes, seeded and chopped
½ cup sliced green onions
3 cups cooked brown rice
½ teaspoon dried rosemary leaves
½ teaspoon salt
½ teaspoon cracked black pepper

Heat oil in large skillet over medium heat until hot. Add lamb and cook 3 to 5 minutes or until lamb is browned. Remove from skillet; reserve. Add squash, mushrooms, tomatoes, and onions; cook 2 to 3 minutes or until vegetables are tender. Stir in rice, rosemary, salt, pepper, and reserved lamb. Cook until thoroughly heated.   *Makes 6 servings*

Each serving provides 258 calories, 19.4 grams protein, 7.6 grams fat, 27.9 grams carbohydrate, 3.5 grams dietary fiber, 313 milligrams sodium, and 50 milligrams cholesterol.

Red Beans and Rice

Vegetable Rice Pizza

3 cups cooked rice
1 egg, beaten
1 cup (4 ounces) shredded
    mozzarella cheese, divided
    Vegetable cooking spray
⅔ cup tomato sauce
2 teaspoons Italian seasoning
¼ teaspoon garlic powder
¼ teaspoon ground black
    pepper

1 tablespoon grated Parmesan
    cheese (optional)
1 cup (about 4 ounces) sliced
    fresh mushrooms
¾ cup thinly sliced zucchini
¼ cup sliced ripe olives
¼ cup diced red pepper
1 tablespoon snipped parsley

Combine rice, egg, and ⅓ cup mozzarella cheese in large bowl. Press into 12-inch pizza pan or 10-inch pie pan coated with cooking spray. Bake at 400°F. for 5 minutes. Combine tomato sauce, Italian seasoning, garlic powder, and black pepper in small bowl; spread over rice crust. Sprinkle with Parmesan cheese. Layer ⅓ cup mozzarella cheese, mushrooms, zucchini, olives, and red pepper. Top with remaining ⅓ cup mozzarella cheese and parsley. Bake at 400°F. for 8 to 10 minutes.

Makes 4 servings

To microwave: Combine rice, egg, and ½ cup mozzarella cheese in large bowl. Press into microproof 12-inch pizza pan or 10-inch pie pan coated with cooking spray. Cook, uncovered, on MEDIUM-HIGH (70% power) 3 to 5 minutes. Combine tomato sauce, Italian seasoning, garlic powder, and black pepper; spread over rice crust. Sprinkle with Parmesan cheese. Layer mushrooms, zucchini, olives, and red pepper. Top with remaining ½ cup mozzarella cheese and parsley. Reduce setting to MEDIUM (50% power) and cook, uncovered, 12 to 15 minutes; rotate dish ¼ turn after 7 minutes. Let stand 5 minutes. (Microwave version has softer texture than conventional version.)

Each serving provides 297 calories, 12.4 grams protein, 9.9 grams fat, 40.8 grams carbohydrate, 4.1 grams dietary fiber, 453 milligrams sodium, and 74 milligrams cholesterol.

Barbecued Shrimp with Spicy Rice

1 pound large shrimp, peeled
  and deveined
4 wooden* or metal skewers

Vegetable cooking spray
⅓ cup prepared barbecue sauce
Spicy Rice (recipe follows)

Thread shrimp on skewers. To broil in oven, place on broiler rack coated with cooking spray. Broil 4 to 5 inches from heat 4 minutes. Brush with barbecue sauce. Turn and brush with remaining barbecue sauce. Broil 2 to 4 minutes longer or until shrimp are done. To cook on outdoor grill, cook skewered shrimp over hot coals 4 minutes. Brush with barbecue sauce. Turn and brush with remaining barbecue sauce. Grill 4 to 5 minutes longer or until shrimp are done. Serve with Spicy Rice.

Makes 4 servings

*Soak wooden skewers in water before using to prevent burning.

Spicy Rice

½ cup sliced green onions
½ cup minced carrots
½ cup minced red pepper
1 jalapeño or serrano pepper,
  minced
1 tablespoon vegetable oil

2 cups cooked rice (cooked in
  chicken broth)
2 tablespoons snipped cilantro
1 tablespoon lime juice
1 teaspoon soy sauce
Hot pepper sauce to taste

Cook onions, carrots, red pepper, and jalapeño pepper in oil in large skillet over medium-high heat until tender crisp. Stir in rice, cilantro, lime juice, soy sauce, and pepper sauce; cook until thoroughly heated. Serve with Barbecued Shrimp.

To microwave: Combine onions, carrots, red pepper, jalapeño pepper, and oil in 2-quart microproof baking dish. Cook on HIGH 2 to 3 minutes or until vegetables are tender crisp. Add rice, cilantro, lime juice, soy sauce, and pepper sauce. Cook on HIGH 3 to 4 minutes, stirring after 2 minutes, or until thoroughly heated. Serve with Barbecued Shrimp.

Each serving provides 285 calories, 22.6 grams protein, 5.2 grams fat, 35.5 grams carbohydrate, 1.9 grams dietary fiber, 839 milligrams sodium, and 175 milligrams cholesterol.

Barbecued Shrimp with Spicy Rice

Quick Skillet Supper

½ pound beef sirloin steak
1 tablespoon vegetable oil
2 cups (about 8 ounces) sliced
    fresh mushrooms
1 can (17 ounces) whole kernel
    corn, drained
1 can (14½ ounces) stewed
    tomatoes, undrained

1 clove garlic, minced
1 teaspoon dried oregano
    leaves
⅛ teaspoon ground black
    pepper
3 cups hot cooked rice

Partially freeze steak; slice across the grain into ⅛-inch strips. Heat oil in large skillet over medium-high heat until hot. Brown meat quickly in oil, about 2 minutes; remove. Add vegetables, garlic, oregano, and pepper; stir. Reduce heat to medium; cover and cook 4 to 6 minutes. Add meat and cook until heated. Serve over rice. *Makes 6 servings*

Each serving provides 288 calories, 14.0 grams protein, 5.3 grams fat, 47.6 grams carbohydrate, 2.1 grams dietary fiber, 694 milligrams sodium, and 23 milligrams cholesterol.

Lemon Rice Stuffed Sole

Vegetable cooking spray
½ cup thinly sliced celery
¼ cup chopped onion
3 cups cooked brown rice
2 teaspoons grated lemon peel
¼ teaspoon salt
¼ teaspoon dried thyme leaves

⅛ teaspoon black pepper
2 tablespoons lemon juice
1 pound fresh or frozen sole
    fillets*
2 teaspoons margarine, melted
1 tablespoon snipped parsley
¼ teaspoon seasoned salt

Coat large skillet with cooking spray and place over medium-high heat until hot. Add celery and onion; cook 2 to 3 minutes or until tender. Stir in rice, lemon peel, salt, thyme, pepper, and lemon juice. Spoon rice mixture on lower portion of each fillet. Fold over to enclose rice mixture; fasten with wooden toothpicks soaked in water. Place remaining rice in bottom of shallow baking dish coated with cooking spray. Place fillets on top of rice. Brush fish with margarine. Sprinkle with parsley and seasoned salt. Bake, uncovered, at 400° F. for 10 to 15 minutes or until fish flakes easily with fork. *Makes 4 servings*

Substitute any white-fleshed fish, such as haddock, turbot, or white fish for the sole, if desired.

Each serving provides 305 calories, 28.2 grams protein, 4.8 grams fat, 35.9 grams carbohydrate, 3.0 grams dietary fiber, 588 milligrams sodium, and 68 milligrams cholesterol.

Brown Rice Chicken Bake

3 cups cooked brown rice
1 package (10 ounces) frozen
   green peas
2 cups cooked chicken breast
   cubes
½ cup cholesterol free, reduced
   calorie mayonnaise
⅓ cup slivered almonds,
   toasted (optional)

2 teaspoons soy sauce
¼ teaspoon ground black
   pepper
¼ teaspoon garlic powder
¼ teaspoon dried tarragon
   leaves
Vegetable cooking spray

Combine rice, peas, chicken, mayonnaise, almonds, soy sauce, and seasonings in bowl. Transfer to 3-quart baking dish coated with cooking spray. Cover and bake at 350° F. for 15 to 20 minutes.   *Makes 6 servings*

Each serving provides 270 calories, 19.6 grams protein, 6.5 grams fat, 32.6 grams carbohydrate, 3.8 grams dietary fiber, 272 milligrams sodium, and 44 milligrams cholesterol.

Paella

1 tablespoon olive oil
½ pound chicken breast cubes
1 cup uncooked rice*
1 medium onion, chopped
1 clove garlic, minced
1½ cups chicken broth
1 can (8 ounces) stewed
   tomatoes, chopped,
   reserving liquid
½ teaspoon paprika

⅛ to ¼ teaspoon ground red
   pepper
⅛ teaspoon ground saffron
½ pound medium shrimp,
   peeled and deveined
1 small red pepper, cut into
   strips
1 small green pepper, cut into
   strips
½ cup frozen green peas

Heat oil in Dutch oven over medium-high heat until hot. Add chicken and stir until browned. Add rice, onion, and garlic. Cook, stirring, until onion is tender and rice is lightly browned. Add broth, tomatoes, tomato liquid, paprika, ground red pepper, and saffron. Bring to a boil; stir. Reduce heat; cover and simmer 10 minutes. Add shrimp, pepper strips, and peas. Cover and simmer 10 minutes or until rice is tender and liquid is absorbed.   *Makes 6 servings*

If using medium grain rice, use 1¼ cups of broth; if using parboiled rice, use 1¾ cups of broth.

Each serving provides 253 calories, 19.8 grams protein, 4.4 grams fat, 32.5 grams carbohydrate, 1.8 grams dietary fiber, 392 milligrams sodium, and 82 milligrams cholesterol.

Rice and Roast Beef Sandwiches

1 small red onion, sliced into
  thin rings
1 teaspoon olive oil
3 cups cooked brown rice
½ cup whole kernel corn
½ cup sliced ripe olives
  (optional)
½ cup barbecue sauce
2 tablespoons lime juice

½ teaspoon ground cumin
½ teaspoon garlic salt
4 whole-wheat pita rounds,
  halved and warmed
8 lettuce leaves
1 cup sliced, cooked lean roast
  beef
1 large tomato, seeded and
  chopped

Cook onion in oil in large skillet over medium-high heat until tender.
Add rice, corn, olives, barbecue sauce, juice, cumin, and garlic salt; toss
until heated. Line each pita half with lettuce leaf, ½ cup hot rice mixture,
and roast beef; top with tomato.   *Makes 8 (½ pita) sandwiches*

Each serving provides 235 calories, 9.3 grams protein, 4.6 grams fat, 37.8 grams
carbohydrate, 4.9 grams dietary fiber, 279 milligrams sodium, and 14 milligrams
cholesterol.

Oriental Fried Rice

3 cups cooked brown rice, cold
½ cup slivered cooked roast
  pork
½ cup finely chopped celery
½ cup fresh bean sprouts*

⅓ cup sliced green onions
1 egg, beaten
Vegetable cooking spray
¼ teaspoon black pepper
2 tablespoons soy sauce

Combine rice, pork, celery, bean sprouts, onions, and egg in large skillet
coated with cooking spray. Cook, stirring, 3 minutes over high heat. Add
pepper and soy sauce. Cook, stirring, 1 minute longer.   *Makes 6 servings*

To microwave: Combine rice, pork, celery, bean sprouts, and onions in
shallow 2-quart microproof baking dish coated with cooking spray. Cook
on HIGH 2 to 3 minutes. Add egg, pepper, and soy sauce. Cook on
HIGH 1 to 2 minutes or until egg is set, stirring to separate grains.

Substitute canned bean sprouts, rinsed and drained, for fresh, if desired.

Each serving provides 156 calories, 7.3 grams protein, 3.4 grams fat, 23.9 grams
carbohydrate, 2.0 grams dietary fiber, 310 milligrams sodium, and 45 milligrams
cholesterol.

*Tip: When preparing fried rice always begin with cold rice. The grains separate
better if cold and it's a great way to use leftover rice.*

Rice and Roast Beef Sandwiches

On the Side

Just when you thought there wasn't another way to prepare rice . . . a collection of great go-alongs.

Almond Brown Rice Stuffing

⅓ cup slivered almonds
2 teaspoons margarine
2 medium tart apples, cored
  and diced
½ cup chopped onion
½ cup chopped celery

½ teaspoon poultry seasoning
¼ teaspoon dried thyme leaves
¼ teaspoon ground white
  pepper
3 cups cooked brown rice
  (cooked in chicken broth)

Cook almonds in margarine in large skillet over medium-high heat until brown. Add apples, onion, celery, poultry seasoning, thyme, and pepper; cook until vegetables are tender crisp. Stir in rice; cook until thoroughly heated. Serve or use as stuffing for poultry or pork roast. Stuffing may be baked in covered baking dish at 375°F. for 15 to 20 minutes.

Makes 6 servings

To microwave: Combine almonds and margarine in 2- to 3-quart microproof baking dish. Cook on HIGH 2 to 3 minutes or until browned. Add apples, onion, celery, poultry seasoning, thyme, and pepper. Cover with waxed paper and cook on HIGH 2 minutes. Stir in rice; cook on HIGH 2 to 3 minutes, stirring after 1½ minutes, or until thoroughly heated. Serve as directed above.

Variations: For Mushroom Stuffing, add 2 cups (about 8 ounces) sliced mushrooms; cook with apples, onion, celery, and seasonings.
For Raisin Stuffing, add ½ cup raisins; cook with apples, onion, celery, and seasonings.

Each serving provides 198 calories, 4.4 grams protein, 6.3 grams fat, 32.5 grams carbohydrate, 4.3 grams dietary fiber, 30 milligrams sodium, and 0 milligram cholesterol.

Almond Brown Rice Stuffing

Arroz Blanco

1 tablespoon margarine
½ cup chopped onion
2 cloves garlic, minced

1 cup uncooked rice*
2 cups chicken broth

Melt margarine in 2- to 3-quart saucepan over medium heat. Add onion and garlic; cook until onion is tender. Add rice and broth. Bring to a boil; stir. Reduce heat; cover and simmer 15 minutes or until rice is tender and liquid is absorbed. Fluff with fork. *Makes 6 servings*

To microwave: Combine margarine, onion, and garlic in deep 2- to 3-quart microproof baking dish. Cover and cook on HIGH 2 minutes. Stir in rice and broth; cover and cook on HIGH 5 minutes. Reduce setting to MEDIUM (50% power) and cook 15 minutes or until rice is tender and liquid is absorbed. Let stand 5 minutes. Fluff with fork.

*Recipe based on regular-milled long grain white rice. If using other types of rice, refer to chart on page 5 for adjustments of liquid and time.

Each serving provides 149 calories, 4.1 grams protein, 2.6 grams fat, 26.3 grams carbohydrate, 0.5 gram dietary fiber, 283 milligrams sodium, and 0 milligram cholesterol.

Tip: Prepare a double batch of Arroz Blanco to have one batch ready for Rice with Tomato and Chiles (page 68) or Green Rice (below) later in the week.

Green Rice

2 Anaheim chiles
1 jalapeño pepper
1 tablespoon margarine or
    olive oil
¼ cup sliced green onions

¼ cup snipped cilantro
1 recipe Arroz Blanco (see
    above)
¼ teaspoon dried oregano
    leaves

Chop chiles and pepper in food processor until minced but not liquid. Melt margarine in large skillet over low heat. Add chiles and cook 1 minute over medium heat. Stir in onions and cilantro; cook 15 to 30 seconds. Add rice mixture and oregano; heat. *Makes 6 servings*

To microwave: Prepare chiles and pepper as directed. Combine chiles, onions, cilantro, and margarine in 2- to 3-quart microproof baking dish. Cook on HIGH 2 to 3 minutes. Add rice mixture and oregano; cover with waxed paper and cook on HIGH 3 minutes, stirring after 2 minutes.

Each serving provides 170 calories, 4.3 grams protein, 4.5 grams fat, 27.3 grams carbohydrate, 0.9 gram dietary fiber, 306 milligrams sodium, and 0 milligram cholesterol.

Clockwise from top: Arroz Blanco, Green Rice, Rice with Tomato and Chiles (page 68)

Rice with Tomato and Chiles

1 green pepper, diced
½ cup chopped onion
1 jalapeño pepper, chopped
1 tablespoon olive oil
1 recipe Arroz Blanco (see page 66)
1 can (14½ ounces) whole tomatoes, drained and chopped

⅛ teaspoon dried oregano leaves
2 tablespoons snipped cilantro for garnish

Cook green pepper, onion, and jalapeño pepper in oil in large skillet over medium-high heat until tender crisp. Stir in rice mixture, tomatoes, and oregano; cook 5 minutes longer. Garnish with cilantro.

Makes 6 servings

To microwave: Combine green pepper, onion, jalapeño pepper, and oil in 2- to 3-quart microproof baking dish. Cook on HIGH 3 to 4 minutes. Add rice mixture, tomatoes, and oregano; cover with waxed paper and cook on HIGH 3 to 4 minutes, stirring after 2 minutes. Garnish with cilantro.

Each serving provides 191 calories, 5.0 grams protein, 5.1 grams fat, 31.2 grams carbohydrate, 1.5 grams dietary fiber, 396 milligrams sodium, and 0 milligram cholesterol.

Tip: To reduce the heat level of jalapeño peppers, scrape and discard the seeds and membranes before chopping.

Harvest Rice

1 cup thinly sliced carrots
1 tablespoon vegetable oil
2 medium apples, cored and chopped
1 cup sliced green onions

3 cups cooked brown rice
½ cup raisins
1 tablespoon sesame seeds, toasted
½ teaspoon salt

Cook carrots in oil in large skillet over medium-high heat until tender crisp. Add apples and onions; cook 5 minutes. Stir in rice, raisins, sesame seeds, and salt. Cook, stirring, until thoroughly heated.

Makes 6 servings

continued

To microwave: Combine carrots and oil in 2-quart microproof baking dish. Cook on HIGH 2 to 3 minutes or until tender crisp. Add apples and onions; continue cooking on HIGH 3 to 4 minutes. Stir in rice, raisins, sesame seeds, and salt. Cover with waxed paper and cook on HIGH 3 to 4 minutes, stirring after 2 minutes, or until thoroughly heated.

Each serving provides 209 calories, 3.8 grams protein, 4.1 grams fat, 41.1 grams carbohydrate, 4.6 grams dietary fiber, 210 milligrams sodium, and 0 milligram cholesterol.

Apricot and Walnut Brown Rice Stuffing

½ cup chopped onion
½ cup chopped celery
1 teaspoon margarine
3 cups cooked brown rice
⅔ cup coarsely chopped dried apricots
¼ cup coarsely chopped walnuts

¼ cup raisins, plumped
2 tablespoons snipped parsley
½ teaspoon dried thyme leaves
¼ teaspoon salt
¼ teaspoon rubbed sage
¼ teaspoon ground black pepper
½ cup chicken broth

Cook onion and celery in margarine in large skillet over medium-high heat until tender crisp. Add rice, apricots, walnuts, raisins, parsley, thyme, salt, sage, pepper, and broth; transfer to 2-quart baking dish. Bake in covered baking dish at 375° F. for 15 to 20 minutes. (Stuffing may be baked inside poultry.) *Makes 6 servings*

To microwave: Reduce chicken broth to ¼ cup. Combine onion, celery, and margarine in 2- to 3-quart microproof baking dish. Cook on HIGH 2 to 3 minutes or until onion is tender. Add rice, apricots, walnuts, raisins, parsley, thyme, salt, sage, pepper, and ¼ cup broth. Cover with waxed paper and cook on HIGH 2 to 3 minutes, stirring after 1½ minutes, or until thoroughly heated.

Each serving provides 183 calories, 4.9 grams protein, 4.7 grams fat, 31.4 grams carbohydrate, 3.2 grams dietary fiber, 185 milligrams sodium, and 0 milligram cholesterol.

Tip: To plump raisins, cover with 1 cup boiling water. Let stand 1 to 2 minutes; drain.

Lemon Rice

1 cup uncooked rice*
1 teaspoon margarine
   (optional)
1 clove garlic, minced
1 teaspoon grated lemon peel

⅛ to ¼ teaspoon ground black
   pepper
2 cups chicken broth
2 tablespoons snipped parsley

Combine rice, margarine, garlic, lemon peel, pepper, and broth in 2- to 3-quart saucepan. Bring to a boil; stir once or twice. Reduce heat; cover and simmer 15 minutes or until rice is tender and liquid is absorbed. Stir in parsley. *Makes 6 servings*

To microwave: Combine rice, margarine, garlic, lemon peel, pepper, and broth in deep 2- to 3-quart microproof baking dish. Cover and cook on HIGH 5 minutes. Reduce setting to MEDIUM (50% power) and cook 15 minutes or until rice is tender and liquid is absorbed. Stir in parsley.

*Recipe based on regular-milled long grain white rice. If using other types of rice, refer to chart on page 5 for adjustments of liquid and time.

Each serving provides 127 calories, 3.9 grams protein, 0.7 gram fat, 25.3 grams carbohydrate, 0.4 gram dietary fiber, 261 grams sodium, and 0 milligram cholesterol.

Walnut Rice

⅓ cup chopped walnuts
¼ to ½ teaspoon red pepper
   flakes
1 teaspoon margarine

3 cups cooked rice (cooked in
   chicken broth)
2 tablespoons grated Parmesan
   cheese
2 tablespoons snipped parsley

Cook walnuts and pepper flakes in margarine in large skillet over medium-high heat until walnuts are lightly browned. Add rice, cheese, and parsley; stir until thoroughly heated. *Makes 6 servings*

To microwave: Combine walnuts, pepper flakes, and margarine in 2-quart microproof baking dish. Cover and cook on HIGH 4 to 5 minutes; stir after 2 minutes. Stir in rice, cheese, and parsley; cook on HIGH 2 to 3 minutes or until thoroughly heated.

Each serving provides 182 calories, 6.3 grams protein, 5.7 grams fat, 26.0 grams carbohydrate, 0.9 gram dietary fiber, 300 milligrams sodium, and 1 milligram cholesterol.

Brown Rice Royal

2 cups (about 8 ounces) sliced
  fresh mushrooms
½ cup thinly sliced green
  onions

1 tablespoon vegetable oil
3 cups cooked brown rice
  (cooked in beef broth)

Cook mushrooms and onions in oil in large skillet over medium-high heat until tender. Add rice. Stir until thoroughly heated.

Makes 6 servings

To microwave: Combine mushrooms, onions, and oil in 2-quart microproof baking dish. Cook on HIGH 2 to 3 minutes. Add rice; continue to cook on HIGH 3 to 4 minutes, stirring after 2 minutes, or until thoroughly heated.

Each serving provides 155 calories, 4.7 grams protein, 3.7 grams fat, 25.7 grams carbohydrate, 1.6 grams dietary fiber, 262 milligrams sodium, and 0 milligram cholesterol.

Spicy Thai Rice

2 cups water
1 cup uncooked rice*
¼ cup chopped green onions
2 fresh red chiles, seeded and
  chopped
1 tablespoon snipped cilantro
1 tablespoon margarine
1 teaspoon minced fresh
  ginger root

¾ teaspoon salt
⅛ teaspoon ground turmeric
1 to 2 teaspoons lime juice
Chopped roasted peanuts for
  garnish (optional)
Red pepper flakes for
  garnish (optional)

Combine water, rice, onions, chiles, cilantro, margarine, ginger root, salt, and turmeric in 2- to 3-quart saucepan. Bring to a boil; stir once or twice. Reduce heat; cover and simmer 15 minutes or until rice is tender and liquid is absorbed. Stir in lime juice; fluff with fork. Garnish with peanuts and pepper flakes.

Makes 6 servings

*Recipe based on regular-milled long grain white rice. If using other types of rice, refer to chart on page 5 for adjustments of liquid and time.

Each serving provides 133 calories, 2.4 grams protein, 1.2 grams fat, 25.4 grams carbohydrate, 0.5 gram dietary fiber, 315 milligrams sodium, and 0 milligram cholesterol.

Brown Rice Royal

Pepper Rice

2 teaspoons vegetable oil	½ cup diced green pepper
1 teaspoon hot chili oil	2 to 3 cloves garlic, minced
½ cup diced red pepper	3 cups cooked rice
½ cup diced yellow pepper	½ teaspoon seasoned salt

Heat oils in large skillet; add peppers and garlic. Cook until tender. Stir in rice and salt. Cook 3 minutes, stirring constantly, until thoroughly heated.

Makes 6 servings

To microwave: Combine oils, peppers, and garlic in 2-quart microproof baking dish. Cook on HIGH 2 to 3 minutes. Add rice and salt; cook on HIGH 2 to 3 minutes or until rice is thoroughly heated.

Each serving provides 164 calories, 3.2 grams protein, 2.7 grams fat, 31.1 grams carbohydrate, 1.1 grams dietary fiber, 588 milligrams sodium, and 0 milligram cholesterol.

Tip: Use lemon juice or toothpaste to remove garlic odor from hands after mincing.

Spanish Rice au Gratin

Vegetable cooking spray	1 teaspoon chili powder
½ cup chopped onion	½ teaspoon Worcestershire sauce
½ cup chopped celery	2 cups cooked brown rice
⅓ cup chopped green pepper	½ cup (2 ounces) shredded Cheddar cheese
1 can (16 ounces) whole tomatoes, drained and chopped	

Coat large skillet with cooking spray and place over medium-high heat until hot. Add onion, celery, and pepper; cook until tender crisp. Add tomatoes, chili powder, and Worcestershire sauce. Stir in rice. Reduce heat; simmer about 5 minutes to blend flavors. Remove from heat. Top with cheese; cover and allow cheese to melt, about 3 minutes.

Makes 4 servings

Each serving provides 204 calories, 7.7 grams protein, 6.0 grams fat, 30.9 grams carbohydrate, 3.5 grams dietary fiber, 314 milligrams sodium, and 15 milligrams cholesterol.

Tip: Add your favorite canned beans, cooked ground beef, or chicken for a main-dish version.

Quick Risotto

2¼ cups chicken broth, divided
1 cup uncooked rice*
  Vegetable cooking spray
½ cup thinly sliced carrots
½ cup thinly sliced yellow
  squash

½ cup thinly sliced zucchini
¼ cup dry white wine
½ cup grated Parmesan cheese
¼ teaspoon ground white
  pepper

Combine 1¾ cups broth and rice in 3-quart saucepan. Bring to a boil; stir once or twice. Reduce heat; cover and simmer 15 minutes or until rice is tender and liquid is absorbed. Coat large skillet with cooking spray and place over medium-high heat until hot. Cook carrots, squash, and zucchini 2 to 3 minutes or until tender crisp. Add wine; cook 2 minutes longer. Set aside and keep warm. Add remaining ½ cup broth to hot rice; stir over medium-high heat until broth is absorbed. Stir in cheese, pepper, and reserved vegetables. Serve immediately.   *Makes 6 servings*

Recipe based on regular-milled medium grain white rice. If using other types of rice, refer to chart on page 5 for adjustments of liquid and time.

Each serving provides 171 calories, 6.9 grams protein, 2.7 grams fat, 28.7 grams carbohydrate, 1.1 grams dietary fiber, 389 milligrams sodium, and 5 milligrams cholesterol.

Tip: Medium grain rice is an excellent choice for risottos.

Rice Primavera

1 clove garlic
2 teaspoons olive oil
2 cups broccoli flowerets
1 cup sliced zucchini
1 cup (about 4 ounces) sliced
  fresh mushrooms
1 medium tomato, seeded and
  chopped

¼ cup snipped parsley
⅓ cup cholesterol free, reduced
  calorie mayonnaise
½ cup skim milk
¼ cup grated Parmesan cheese
¼ teaspoon ground white or
  ground red pepper
3 cups hot cooked rice

Heat garlic in oil in large skillet over medium-high heat; remove and discard garlic. Cook broccoli, zucchini, and mushrooms in oil until almost tender crisp. Add tomato and parsley; cook 1 minute longer. Remove vegetables; set aside. Place mayonnaise in same skillet; stir in milk, cheese, and pepper. Cook over medium heat, stirring until smooth. Add rice; toss to coat. Stir in vegetables; heat.   *Makes 6 servings*

Each serving provides 234 calories, 7.2 grams protein, 7.2 grams fat, 35.6 grams carbohydrate, 2.5 grams dietary fiber, 552 milligrams sodium, and 8 milligrams cholesterol.

Spinach Feta Rice

1 cup uncooked rice*
1 cup chicken broth
1 cup water
1 medium onion, chopped
1 cup (about 4 ounces) sliced
   fresh mushrooms
2 cloves garlic, minced
   Vegetable cooking spray
1 tablespoon lemon juice

½ teaspoon dried oregano
   leaves
6 cups shredded fresh spinach
   leaves (about ¼ pound)
4 ounces feta cheese, crumbled
   Freshly ground black pepper
   Chopped pimiento for
   garnish (optional)

Combine rice, broth, and water in medium saucepan. Bring to a boil; stir once or twice. Reduce heat; cover and simmer 15 minutes or until rice is tender and liquid is absorbed. Cook onion, mushrooms, and garlic in large skillet coated with cooking spray until onion is tender. Stir in lemon juice and oregano. Add spinach, cheese, pepper, and rice; toss lightly until spinach is wilted. Garnish with pimiento.   *Makes 6 servings*

To microwave: Combine rice, broth, and water in deep 2- to 3-quart microproof baking dish. Cover and cook on HIGH 5 minutes. Reduce setting to MEDIUM (50% power) and cook 15 minutes or until rice is tender and liquid is absorbed. Combine onion, mushrooms, and garlic in 1-quart microproof baking dish coated with cooking spray. Cook on HIGH 2 to 3 minutes. Add vegetables, lemon juice, oregano, spinach, cheese, and pepper to hot cooked rice. Cook on HIGH 1 to 2 minutes or until spinach is wilted. Garnish with pimiento.

Recipe based on regular-milled long grain white rice. If using other types of rice, refer to chart on page 5 for adjustments of liquid and time.

Each serving provides 195 calories, 7.9 grams protein, 4.8 grams fat, 30.4 grams carbohydrate, 3.1 grams dietary fiber, 387 milligrams sodium, and 17 milligrams cholesterol.

Antipasto Rice

1½ cups water
½ cup tomato juice
1 cup uncooked rice*
1 teaspoon dried basil leaves
1 teaspoon dried oregano
   leaves
½ teaspoon salt (optional)
1 can (14 ounces) artichoke
   hearts, drained and
   quartered

1 jar (7 ounces) roasted red
   peppers, drained and
   chopped
1 can (2¼ ounces) sliced ripe
   olives, drained
2 tablespoons snipped parsley
2 tablespoons lemon juice
½ teaspoon ground black
   pepper
2 tablespoons grated Parmesan
   cheese

Combine water, tomato juice, rice, basil, oregano, and salt in 2- to 3-quart saucepan. Bring to a boil; stir once or twice. Reduce heat; cover and simmer 15 minutes or until rice is tender and liquid is absorbed. Stir in artichokes, red peppers, olives, parsley, lemon juice, and black pepper. Cook 5 minutes longer or until thoroughly heated. Sprinkle with cheese.

Makes 8 servings

To microwave: Combine water, tomato juice, rice, basil, oregano, and salt in deep 2- to 3-quart microproof baking dish. Cover and cook on HIGH 5 minutes. Reduce setting to MEDIUM (50% power) and cook 15 minutes or until rice is tender and liquid is absorbed. Add artichokes, red peppers, olives, parsley, lemon juice, and black pepper. Cook on HIGH 2 to 3 minutes or until mixture is thoroughly heated. Sprinkle with cheese.

Recipe based on regular-milled long grain white rice. For medium grain rice, use 1¼ cups water and cook for 15 minutes. For parboiled rice, use 1¾ cups water and cook for 20 to 25 minutes. For brown rice, use 1¾ cups water and cook for 45 to 50 minutes.

Each serving provides 131 calories, 3.7 grams protein, 1.6 grams fat, 26.5 grams carbohydrate, 1.3 grams dietary fiber, 522 milligrams sodium, and 1 milligram cholesterol.

Antipasto Rice

Oriental Rice Pilaf

½ cup chopped onion
1 clove garlic, minced
1 tablespoon sesame oil
1¾ cups beef broth
1 cup uncooked rice*
1 tablespoon reduced-sodium
   soy sauce

⅛ to ¼ teaspoon red pepper
   flakes
⅓ cup thinly sliced green
   onions
⅓ cup diced red pepper
2 tablespoons sesame seeds,
   toasted

Cook onion and garlic in oil in 2- to 3-quart saucepan over medium heat until onion is tender. Add broth, rice, soy sauce, and pepper flakes. Bring to a boil; stir once or twice. Reduce heat; cover and simmer 15 to 20 minutes or until rice is tender and liquid is absorbed. Stir green onions, red pepper, and sesame seeds into cooked rice; cover and let stand 5 minutes. Fluff with fork.   *Makes 6 servings*

Recipe based on regular-milled long grain white rice. If using other types of rice, refer to chart on page 5 for adjustments of liquid and time.

Each serving provides 168 calories, 4.6 grams protein, 4.2 grams fat, 28.1 grams carbohydrate, 0.9 gram dietary fiber, 312 milligrams sodium, and 7 milligrams cholesterol.

Southwestern Vegetable Rice

2 cups chicken broth
1 cup uncooked rice*
⅔ cup diced green pepper
⅔ cup chopped tomato
½ cup chopped onion

1 tablespoon margarine
1 teaspoon chili powder
1 teaspoon ground cumin
¼ teaspoon ground red pepper

Combine all ingredients in 2- to 3-quart saucepan. Bring to a boil; stir once or twice. Reduce heat; cover and simmer 15 minutes or until rice is tender and liquid is absorbed. Fluff with fork.   *Makes 6 servings*

To microwave: Combine all ingredients in deep 2- to 3-quart microproof baking dish. Cover and cook on HIGH 5 minutes. Reduce setting to MEDIUM (50% power); cook 15 minutes or until rice is tender and liquid is absorbed. Fluff with fork.

Recipe based on regular-milled long grain white rice. If using other types of rice, refer to chart on page 5 for adjustments of liquid and time.

Each serving provides 158 calories, 4.4 grams protein, 2.9 grams fat, 28.2 grams carbohydrate, 1.3 grams dietary fiber, 290 milligrams sodium, and 0 milligram cholesterol.

Oriental Rice Pilaf

Health Nut Brown Rice

½ cup shredded carrot
½ cup shredded zucchini
3 tablespoons sunflower
   kernels
3 tablespoons sliced almonds
¼ teaspoon red pepper flakes
   (optional)

1 teaspoon margarine
3 cups cooked brown rice
   (cooked in chicken broth)
2 tablespoons snipped parsley

Cook carrot, zucchini, sunflower kernels, almonds, and pepper flakes in margarine in large skillet over medium-high heat until almonds are browned. Add rice and parsley; stir until heated. *Makes 6 servings*

To microwave: Combine carrot, zucchini, sunflower kernels, almonds, pepper flakes, and margarine in 2-quart microproof baking dish. Cook on HIGH 3 to 4 minutes or until almonds are lightly browned. Add rice and parsley; cook on HIGH 3 to 4 minutes, stirring after 2 minutes, or until heated.

Each serving provides 182 calories, 5.9 grams protein, 5.8 grams fat, 26.9 grams carbohydrate, 2.1 grams dietary fiber, 273 milligrams sodium, and 0 milligram cholesterol.

Risotto with Peas and Mushrooms

½ cup chopped onion
2 teaspoons margarine
1 cup uncooked rice
⅓ cup dry white wine
1 cup chicken broth
4 cups water
1 cup frozen peas, thawed

1 jar (2½ ounces) sliced
   mushrooms, drained
¼ cup grated Parmesan cheese
¼ teaspoon ground white
   pepper
⅓ cup 2% low-fat milk

Cook onion in margarine in large skillet over medium-high heat until soft. Add rice; stir 2 to 3 minutes. Add wine; stir until absorbed. Stir in broth. Cook, uncovered, stirring constantly, until broth is absorbed. Continue stirring and adding water, one cup at a time; allow each cup to be absorbed before adding another, until rice is tender and has a creamy consistency, 20 to 25 minutes. Stir in remaining ingredients. Stir until creamy, 1 to 2 minutes. Serve immediately. *Makes 6 servings*

Each serving provides 205 calories, 6.7 grams protein, 5.6 grams fat, 31.3 grams carbohydrate, 1.8 grams dietary fiber, 316 milligrams sodium, and 4 milligrams cholesterol.

Tip: Medium grain rice will yield the best consistency for risottos, but long grain rice can be used.

Stuffed Squash

6 small acorn squash, about
 ½ pound each
2 cups cooked rice
1 medium tart apple, cored
 and diced
½ cup finely chopped green
 onions
½ cup chopped celery
½ cup chopped dates

¼ cup rice bran (optional)
¼ cup chopped walnuts
2 tablespoons lemon juice
2 tablespoons margarine,
 melted
½ teaspoon ground cinnamon
¼ teaspoon ground nutmeg
4 gingersnap cookies, crushed
 (optional)

To microwave: Pierce squash with meat fork in two places. Cook on
HIGH 12 to 14 minutes or until just tender, turning squash over after
6 minutes. (Do not overcook.) Let stand 5 minutes. Cut in half and scoop
out seeds. Combine rice and remaining ingredients except cookies in large
bowl; mix lightly. Spoon rice mixture into squash halves; place on round
microproof dish. Cover tightly with vented plastic wrap. Cook on HIGH
4 to 6 minutes or until thoroughly heated. Sprinkle with gingersnap
crumbs before serving. *Makes 6 servings*

Each serving provides 341 calories, 6.3 grams protein, 7.5 grams fat, 68.6 grams
carbohydrate, 5.8 grams dietary fiber, 324 milligrams sodium, and 0 milligram
cholesterol.

Pesto Rice and Vegetables

1½ cups packed basil, arugula,
 watercress, or spinach
 leaves
1 clove garlic
⅓ cup grated Parmesan cheese
1 tablespoon olive oil

Vegetable cooking spray
1½ cups broccoli flowerets
1 cup sliced carrots
3 cups cooked brown or white
 rice

Finely mince basil and garlic in food processor. Add cheese and oil. Pulse
until combined; scrape bowl as necessary. Coat large skillet with cooking
spray; place over medium-high heat until hot. Cook vegetables until
tender crisp. Stir in rice and basil mixture. Serve immediately.

Makes 6 servings

To microwave: Prepare basil mixture as directed above. Combine broccoli
and carrots in 2-quart microproof baking dish. Cover and cook on HIGH
2 minutes; stir. Cook on HIGH 1 to 1½ minutes longer or until vegetables
are tender crisp. Stir in rice and basil mixture. Cover and cook on HIGH
1½ to 2½ minutes, stirring every minute, or until hot. Serve immediately.

Each serving provides 166 calories, 5.4 grams protein, 4.6 grams fat, 26.4 grams
carbohydrate, 3.0 grams dietary fiber, 102 milligrams sodium, and 4 milligrams
cholesterol.

Healthy Temptations

Indulge with these taste-tempting rice dessert recipes that are low in calories and fat.

Rice Crêpes

1 carton (8 ounces) egg
    substitute*
⅔ cup evaporated skim milk
1 tablespoon margarine,
    melted
½ cup all-purpose flour
1 tablespoon sugar
1 cup cooked rice
    Vegetable cooking spray

2½ cups fresh fruit
    (strawberries, raspberries,
    blueberries, or other
    favorite fruit)
Low-sugar fruit spread
    (optional)
Light sour cream (optional)
1 tablespoon confectioner's
    sugar for garnish
    (optional)

Combine egg substitute, milk, and margarine in small bowl. Stir in flour and sugar until smooth and well blended. Stir in rice; let stand 5 minutes. Heat 8-inch nonstick skillet or crêpe pan; coat with cooking spray. Spoon ¼ cup batter into pan. Lift pan off heat; quickly tilt pan in rotating motion so that bottom of pan is completely covered with batter. Place pan back on heat and continue cooking until surface is dry, about 45 seconds. Turn crêpe over and cook 15 to 20 seconds; set aside. Continue with remaining crêpe batter. Place waxed paper between crêpes. Spread each crêpe with your favorite filling: strawberries, raspberries, blueberries, fruit spread, or sour cream. Roll up and sprinkle with confectioner's sugar for garnish.
Makes 10 crêpes

Substitute 8 egg whites or 4 eggs for 1 carton (8 ounces) egg substitute, if desired.

Each serving provides 111 calories, 5.4 grams protein, 2.2 grams fat, 17.2 grams carbohydrate, 1.2 grams dietary fiber, 152 milligrams sodium, and 1 milligram cholesterol.

Rice Crêpes

Bavarian Rice Cloud with Bittersweet Chocolate Sauce

1 envelope unflavored gelatin
1½ cups skim milk
3 tablespoons sugar
2 cups cooked rice
2 cups frozen light whipped topping, thawed
1 tablespoon almond-flavored liqueur

½ teaspoon vanilla extract
Vegetable cooking spray
Bittersweet Chocolate Sauce (recipe follows)
2 tablespoons sliced almonds, toasted

Sprinkle gelatin over milk in small saucepan; let stand 1 minute or until gelatin is softened. Cook over low heat, stirring constantly, until gelatin dissolves. Add sugar and stir until dissolved. Add rice; stir until well blended. Cover and chill until the consistency of unbeaten egg whites. Fold in whipped topping, liqueur, and vanilla. Spoon into 4-cup mold coated with cooking spray. Cover and chill until firm. To serve, unmold onto serving platter. Spoon chocolate sauce over rice dessert. Sprinkle with toasted almonds. *Makes 10 servings*

Bittersweet Chocolate Sauce

3 tablespoons cocoa
3 tablespoons sugar
½ cup low-fat buttermilk

1 tablespoon almond-flavored liqueur

Combine cocoa and sugar in small saucepan. Add buttermilk, mixing well. Place over medium heat, and cook until sugar dissolves. Stir in liqueur; remove from heat.

Each serving provides 146 calories, 4.2 grams protein, 3.1 grams fat, 24.7 grams carbohydrate, 0.4 gram dietary fiber, 211 milligrams sodium, and 1 milligram cholesterol.

Tip: Unmold gelatin desserts onto slightly dampened plate. This will allow you to move the mold and position it where you want it on the plate.

Bavarian Rice Cloud with Bittersweet Chocolate Sauce

Chocolate Fruit Crispies

6 cups crisp rice cereal
½ cup raisins
½ cup finely chopped dried
   apricots
1 bag (10 ounces) large
   marshmallows (about 40)

½ cup (3 ounces) semisweet
   chocolate morsels
2 tablespoons milk
Vegetable cooking spray

Combine cereal, raisins, and apricots in large bowl; set aside. Combine marshmallows, chocolate, and milk in 2-quart saucepan. Place over low heat and cook, stirring, about 10 minutes or until melted. Pour over cereal mixture; mix well. Coat 12×8×2-inch baking pan with cooking spray; spread mixture evenly into pan. Press down firmly using fingers coated with cooking spray. Cover and chill until firm. Cut into 1-inch squares.

Makes 8 dozen crispies

To microwave: Combine cereal, raisins, and apricots in large bowl; set aside. Combine marshmallows, chocolate, and milk in 1½-quart microproof dish. Cook, uncovered, on HIGH 1 minute; stir until smooth. Continue as directed above.

Each crispy provides 25 calories, 0.3 gram protein, 0.3 gram fat, 5.5 grams carbohydrate, 0.1 gram dietary fiber, 24 milligrams sodium, and 0 milligram cholesterol.

Tip: A great low-fat snack!

Raspberry Rice aux Amandes

3 cups cooked rice
2 cups skim milk
⅛ teaspoon salt
   Low-calorie sugar substitute
     to equal 2 tablespoons
     sugar
1 teaspoon vanilla extract

¾ cup frozen light whipped
   topping, thawed
3 tablespoons sliced almonds,
   toasted
1 package (16 ounces) frozen
   unsweetened raspberries,
   thawed*

Combine rice, milk, and salt in 2-quart saucepan. Cook over medium heat until thick and creamy, 5 to 8 minutes, stirring frequently. Remove from heat. Cool. Add sugar substitute and vanilla. Fold in whipped topping and almonds. Alternate rice mixture and raspberries in parfait glasses or dessert dishes.

Makes 8 servings

Substitute frozen unsweetened strawberries or other fruit for the raspberries, if desired.

continued

To microwave: Combine rice, milk, and salt in 1½-quart microproof baking dish. Cover and cook on HIGH 3 minutes. Reduce setting to MEDIUM (50% power) and cook 7 minutes, stirring after 3 and 5 minutes. Stir in sugar substitute and vanilla; cool. Fold in whipped topping and almonds. Alternate rice mixture and raspberries in parfait glasses or dessert dishes.

Each serving provides 180 calories, 5.4 grams protein, 2.6 grams fat, 33.1 grams carbohydrate, 4.8 grams dietary fiber, 369 milligrams sodium, and 2 milligrams cholesterol.

Fresh Fruit Tart

3 cups cooked rice
¼ cup sugar
1 egg, beaten
   Vegetable cooking spray
1 package (8 ounces) light cream cheese, softened
¼ cup plain nonfat yogurt
¼ cup confectioner's sugar

1 teaspoon vanilla extract
⅓ cup low-sugar apricot or peach spread
1 tablespoon water
2 to 3 cups fresh fruit (sliced strawberries, raspberries, blueberries, sliced kiwifruit, grape halves)

Combine rice, sugar, and egg in medium bowl. Press into 12-inch pizza pan or 10-inch pie pan coated with cooking spray. Bake at 350°F. for 10 minutes. Cool.

Beat cream cheese and yogurt in medium bowl until light and fluffy. Add confectioner's sugar and vanilla; beat until well blended. Spread over crust.

Heat apricot spread and water in small saucepan over low heat. Strain; cool. Brush half of glaze over filling. Arrange fruit attractively over crust, starting at outer edge. Brush remaining glaze evenly over fruit. Cover and chill 1 to 2 hours before serving. *Makes 8 servings*

Each serving provides 257 calories, 6.4 grams protein, 7.6 grams fat, 40.6 grams carbohydrate, 1.4 grams dietary fiber, 432 milligrams sodium, and 48 milligrams cholesterol.

Blueberry Crisp

3 cups cooked brown rice
3 cups fresh blueberries*
¼ cup + 3 tablespoons firmly
    packed brown sugar,
    divided
Vegetable cooking spray

⅓ cup rice bran
¼ cup whole-wheat flour
¼ cup chopped walnuts
1 teaspoon ground cinnamon
3 tablespoons margarine

Combine rice, blueberries, and 3 tablespoons sugar. Coat 8 individual custard cups or 2-quart baking dish with cooking spray. Place rice mixture in cups or baking dish; set aside. Combine bran, flour, walnuts, remaining ¼ cup sugar, and cinnamon in bowl. Cut in margarine with pastry blender until mixture resembles coarse meal. Sprinkle over rice mixture. Bake at 375° F. for 15 to 20 minutes or until thoroughly heated. Serve warm. *Makes 8 servings*

To microwave: Prepare as directed using 2-quart microproof baking dish. Cook, uncovered, on HIGH 4 to 5 minutes, rotating dish once during cooking time. Let stand 5 minutes. Serve warm.

*Substitute frozen unsweetened blueberries for the fresh blueberries, if desired. Thaw and drain before using. Or, substitute your choice of fresh fruit or combinations of fruit for the blueberries, if desired.

Each serving provides 243 calories, 3.8 grams protein, 8.2 grams fat, 41.5 grams carbohydrate, 4.3 grams dietary fiber, 61 milligrams sodium, and 0 milligram cholesterol.

Banana-Kiwi Pudding

1⅓ cups cooked rice
1⅓ cups skim milk
1 teaspoon vanilla extract
    Low-calorie sugar substitute
    to equal 2 tablespoons
    sugar

1 ripe banana
¼ cup whipping cream,
    whipped
2 kiwifruit, sliced, for garnish

Cook rice and milk in 2-quart saucepan over medium heat until thick and creamy, 5 to 8 minutes, stirring frequently. Remove from heat; cool. Stir in vanilla and sugar substitute. Just before serving, mash banana; fold banana and whipped cream into pudding. Garnish with kiwifruit slices. *Makes 4 servings*

Each serving provides 197 calories, 5.6 grams protein, 3.5 grams fat, 35.3 grams carbohydrate, 2.0 grams dietary fiber, 306 milligrams sodium, and 12 milligrams cholesterol.

Blueberry Crisp

Rice Pudding

3 cups 2% low-fat milk
1 large stick cinnamon
1 cup uncooked rice*
2 cups water
½ teaspoon salt

Peel of an orange or lemon
¾ cup sugar
¼ cup raisins
2 tablespoons dark rum

Heat milk and cinnamon in small saucepan over medium heat until milk is infused with flavor of cinnamon, about 15 minutes. Combine rice, water, and salt in 2- to 3-quart saucepan. Bring to a boil; stir once or twice. Place orange peel on top of rice. Reduce heat; cover and simmer 15 minutes or until rice is tender and liquid is absorbed. Remove and discard orange peel. Strain milk and stir into cooked rice. Add sugar and simmer 20 minutes or until thickened, stirring often. Add raisins and rum; simmer 10 minutes. Serve hot. To reheat, add a little milk to restore creamy texture. *Makes 6 servings*

*Recipe based on regular-milled long grain white rice. If using other types of rice, refer to chart on page 5 for adjustments of liquid and time.

Each serving provides 297 calories, 6.4 grams protein, 2.6 grams fat, 62.5 grams carbohydrate, 0.6 gram dietary fiber, 259 milligrams sodium, and 10 milligrams cholesterol.

Tip: Use medium or short grain rice for rice pudding with a creamier consistency.

Lemon Rice Dessert

1 package (3 ounces) lemon-
  flavored gelatin dessert
1 cup boiling water
½ cup cold water
1 cup cooked rice, chilled

1½ cups frozen whipped
  topping, thawed
¼ cup sliced almonds
¼ cup chopped maraschino
  cherries
1 tablespoon grated lemon peel

Dissolve gelatin in boiling water; add cold water. Place bowl in ice water and stir until gelatin is the consistency of unbeaten egg whites; stir in rice. Fold in whipped topping until smooth. Lightly fold in almonds, cherries, and lemon peel. Continue to stir gently (over ice) until thickened. Pour into dessert dishes. Cover and chill until ready to serve. *Makes 8 servings*

Each serving provides 131 calories, 2.6 grams protein, 3.3 grams fat, 22.6 grams carbohydrate, 0.5 gram dietary fiber, 149 milligrams sodium, and 2 milligrams cholesterol.

Rice Pudding

Index